# Out of
# SLAVERY

*Learning about the history
of black British Caribbean people*

**Nardia Foster**

Redcliffe

## Acknowledgements

The publisher gratefully acknowledges the following for permission to reproduce copyright material:

*Text*
Fryer, Peter, *Staying Power: Black People in Britain since 1504*, Pluto, 1984
Karenga, Maulana, *Introduction to Black Studies*, University of Sankore Press, Los Angeles
Sheridan, R. B., *Doctors and Slaves*, Cambridge University Press, 1985

*Images*
The author, pages 28, 29.
The Bridgeman Art Library, front cover (left), pages 16, 17, 18 (bottom), 30, 37, 38, 45, 46 (bottom), 49, 50 (top and bottom), 51, 55 (top and bottom), 62, 64, 65, 67, 72, 73, 74, 80, 87, 88, 89 (top), 90, 92, 94, 96, 99 (top), 103, 115, 119.
The College of Arms, page 113.
Corbis, pages 54, 59, 60, 70, 83, 97, 99 (bottom), 132, 141, 142, 144.
The J. Paul Getty Museum, Villa Collection, Malibu, California, page 22.
Grant Lynch, front cover (2nd and 3rd from left).
The Imperial War Museum, front cover (2nd from right), pages 123, 127 (top and bottom), 128.
Mary Evans Picture Library, page 108, 133.
The National Library of Jamaica, page 82.
The National Maritime Museum, page 46 (top).
National Museums Liverpool, Merseyside Maritime Museum, page 89 (bottom).
The National Portrait Gallery, pages 114, 116, 120.
The Public Record Office, page 131.

Every effort has been made to trace copyright holders and to obtain their permission for the use for copyright material. The author and publisher will gladly receive information enabling them to rectify any error or omission in subsequent editions.

Published by Redcliffe Publishing
49 Jessop Court, Ferry Street, Buchanans Wharf, Bristol BS1 6HP

First printed 2004

ISBN 0-9547420-0-1

# Contents

# Preface

There was a time in Britain – about a hundred years ago – when black people (and those of other racial groups) were regarded as something less than human. Although, thankfully, such extreme forms of racism are no longer acceptable in our society, there are clearly problems connected with the issue of race in Britain at the beginning of the twenty-first century. In the BBC's 2003 Race Survey, a third of black people said they had faced racism at school or in further or higher education, and half of all respondents believed that Britain is a racist society.

There are specific issues within education: particular concern surrounds the children from families of black African and Caribbean origin – who seem to be failed by an education system that leaves them disaffected and with unfulfilled potential. In one survey, the percentage of black children achieving five or more GCSEs was 36 per cent, as compared with 52 per cent of white children and 60 per cent of Indian children. Trevor Phillips, chair of the Commission for Racial Equality, observed, 'The lack of attainment is not just disturbing, but is now repeating itself from generation to generation'.

There are many initiatives aimed at addressing the problem. Meanwhile, schools are being encouraged to incorporate black history into the curriculum and to become involved in activities such as the annual Black History Month. My personal involvement began some years ago when a teacher colleague asked if I could conduct a workshop on black history at her school. As I set about preparing for it, I was concerned to find that the only readily available material was about American black history. So began my research into black British history that took three and a half years.

As I began to work with other schools, it became apparent that most teachers knew very little about black history generally, and less still about the history of British people of Caribbean descent. Often, attention is given to the history of American black people and the civil rights movement, while that of British black people is largely neglected. Given that American history is well supported by curriculum texts, while the British part of the story has virtually none, perhaps this is not surprising. Within the flexible framework of the History National Curriculum, there is plenty of scope for studying black British history, but little in the way of suitable teaching material. *Out of Slavery* is an attempt to provide a remedy for that situation.

While this book is designed to cater for the needs of teachers and schools, it was also written with a wider audience very much in mind. It is therefore presented not simply as a curriculum text, but as an accessible historical account and a flexible resource that will be useful to anyone with a professional or personal interest in the black presence in Britain. Above all, this book aims to help dispel ignorance about British Caribbean people and to foster the type of understanding that is the basis of a fair and just society for peoples of all races.

There are many people I would like to thank for being instrumental in the writing of this book, beginning with Jean James, the teacher who invited me to hold that first workshop on black history. My sincere thanks also to those who have subsequently invited me to take INSET training, workshops and seminars, especially: Sir James Barrie Primary School, London; St James Primary Church of England School, Essex, who have allowed me to take part in their Arts Week over several years, teaching in all subject areas about black British history; Surrey County Council; The Professional Association of Teachers. Thanks also to The Nehemiah Trust, with whom I collaborated on a quiz for Birmingham schools in Black History Month, 2003.

I am grateful to the many people whose help and encouragement has meant so much to me during the research, including: Yasmin Valli (Leeds University), Nicola Rollock (Runnymede), Shiraz Chakera of the GTC, Professor David Gillborn (Institute of Education), Marika Sherwood (Institute of Commonwealth Studies), Heidi Safia Mirza (Middlesex University), Marcia Sinclair of Enfield, Albert Smith (MaPS LTD), Linda Appiah, Joan Foulds (Cambridgeshire County Council), Sonia Hall of the CRE, Jerome Freeman of the QCA, and all those at Tramway, Edmonton. Thanks also to Sara Grove of The Bridgeman Art Library, who was so supportive of the idea for this book and helpful in the picture research. Finally, thanks to Captain David Horn, Curator of The Guards Museum who gave me access to the books and artwork of black guardsmen.

My thanks also to Elaine Arnold for taking photographs in Jamaica, and to all the people who allowed me to interview them about their experiences. A special thank you to my sisters, especially the Reverend Doreen Morrison, who had to put up with all my thoughts and ideas about the book, and to the team who put it together with Paul Uttley, the publisher, a man of vision.

And finally to my family, my loving and encouraging children, Sarah, David and Esther, and to my husband who has been waiting eagerly for the final results.

I hope the reader will enjoy this book as much as I enjoyed writing it.

*Nardia Foster 2004*

# Introduction

Britain has always been inhabited by migrant people. Most of us living on these islands are either immigrants or descended from immigrants. British history is a story of comings and goings. It is this mixing of races and cultures that has made Britain such a rich country. It is recognised that ethnic diversity has contributed much in every area of life – the arts, science, technology, industry and commerce.

Nevertheless, not all immigrants have been welcomed, and people of different races have not always been treated with equal respect. The experience of ethnic minorities has sometimes been a bitter one.

Of the 4.6 million British people who belong to a minority ethnic community, one million are of either black African or black Caribbean origin, and the largest single group is that whose origins are in the Caribbean, also known as the West Indies. The story of how these people came to live in Britain stretches back over 500 years and is deeply connected with the histories of Britain and other European countries.

At the heart of the story is the Atlantic slave trade, a dark episode of history that has attracted a good deal of curiosity: the scale of the cruelty and human suffering spanning more than two centuries holds a grim fascination. On another level, the slave trade had profound and lasting consequences on three continents. In Africa, it left whole states ravaged to the point of collapse; the Americas were transformed by a significant population of African slaves; and Europe reaped the benefits of material prosperity. Slavery affected the economic and political life of all these continents, setting patterns for relations of power, some of which endure to this day.

Slavery also created a people whose identity was forged out of oppression. It set up patterns of relationship between black people and white people that have been the cause of open conflict and immeasurable suffering. We do not have to go back very far in British history to read about legislation that discriminated on racial grounds, race riots and vicious racial attacks. Nearly two centuries after the abolition of slavery, the ripples are still spreading out.

## Why this book?

For any society to move forward in the right direction, it is important to know the story so far, and to understand the reasons behind the current state of affairs.

This book tells the story of black British Caribbean people and their journey from Africa to Britain. In recent years, the slave trade and related topics have attracted a great deal of interest among historical researchers and there are many excellent scholarly works on the subject. This book, however, is not an academic work, but it draws on recent research and primary source material to offer a clear and accessible overview – not only of the transatlantic slave trade, but of the whole story so far, from its beginnings in Africa to post-war immigration and the race riots of the last century.

Through telling the story, it examines the deep connections between Britain, Africa and the Caribbean, and explores some of the important questions, such as: What were the economic and social conditions that led to the establishment of the slave trade? How were ordinary white people able to accept slavery as a way of life for so long? How were people able to treat people of another race with such contempt and cruelty? What were the effects of slavery on subsequent generations of African–Caribbeans? What patterns persist in the relationship between white British and black British people?

Most importantly, the aim is neither to apportion blame nor to excuse; it is simply to increase understanding of the present through an awareness of the past. When the events of the past are read with honesty, the future can be faced with more hope. The historical events described here should be included in the education of all British citizens.

## Who is it for?

This is a resource for all schools and all educators.

In the classroom, it supports the National Curriculum for History, and is especially relevant to the Core Study Unit Britain 1750–1900 at Key Stage 3.

It includes many textual and visual sources, as well as questions and suggestions for further research that will encourage students to reflect on the wider issues and implications. Some sections will also be relevant to topics within English, PSHE and citizenship. (See the table on page 12 for more details of curriculum links.)

In the staffroom, it can provide a source of invaluable reference for anyone working with children of black Caribbean origin.

While the book has been written with teachers and students particularly in mind, this by no means excludes a wider audience – as it provides a readable and accessible account for anyone interested in Caribbean people and their remarkable history.

# National Curriculum links

*Items from the National Curriculum notes on examples are given in italics.*

### Key Stage 2

| History Programme of Study | Relates to chapters |
|---|---|
| **History**<br>**Britain and the wider world in Tudor Times**<br>*traders and settlers; trade with Africa, Asia and America* | 4 Conquest and cultivation<br>5 Capture and deportation<br>6 Life on the plantations<br>7 Slave communities and culture |
| **Victorian Britain**<br>*Mary Seacole and the Crimean War* | 12 Black presence in Britain<br>    up to 1900 |

| PSHE and Citizenship Programme of Study | Relates to chapters |
|---|---|
| **Knowledge, skills and understanding** | |
| – to realise the consequences of antisocial and aggressive behaviours, such as bullying and racism, on individuals and communities | 14 Post-war migrants and settlers<br>15 Born black, born British |
| – to reflect on spiritual, moral, social and cultural issues, using imagination to understand other people's experiences | All |
| – to appreciate the range of national, regional, religious and ethnic identities in the United Kingdom | 14 Post-war migrants and settlers<br>15 Born black, born British |
| **Developing good relationships and respecting the differences between people** | |
| – to think about the lives of people living in other places and times, and people with different values and customs | All |
| – to realise the nature and consequences of racism, teasing, bullying and aggressive behaviours, and how to respond to them and ask for help | 15 Born black, born British |

| – to recognise and challenge stereotypes | 15 Born black, born British |
|---|---|
| – that differences and similarities between people arise from a number of factors, including cultural, ethnic, racial and religious diversity, gender and disability | All |

## Other subject links

- English: Reading: Literature – texts drawn from a variety of cultures and traditions.
- Music: a range of live and recorded music from different times and cultures.

### Key Stage 3

| History Programme of Study | Relates to chapters |
|---|---|
| **A world study before 1900** – the study of the culture, beliefs and achievement of an African society | 1 African roots |
| **Britain 1750–1900** – expansion of trade and colonisation | 4 Conquest and cultivation<br>5 Capture and deportation<br>6 Life on the plantations<br>7 Slave communities and culture |
| **Britain 1750–1900** – political changes<br>– the abolition of slavery and the slave trade in the British Empire, and the work of reformers such as William Wilberforce and Olaudah Equiano | 9 Ending the trade<br>10 The fight for freedom<br>11 Loosing the shackles |
| **A world study after 1900** – some of the significant individuals, events and developments from across the twentieth century | 13 Black people in wartime<br>14 Post-war migrants and settlers<br>15 Born black, born British |

| Citizenship Programme of Study | Relates to chapters |
|---|---|
| **Knowledge and understanding about becoming informed citizens**<br>– the legal and human rights and responsibilities underpinning society | 2 Slavery |
| – the diversity of national, regional, religious and ethnic identities in the United Kingdom and the need for mutual respect and understanding | 13 Black people in wartime<br>14 Post-war migrants and settlers<br>15 Born black, born British |

| | |
|---|---|
| – the importance of resolving conflict fairly | 15 Born black, born British |
| – the world as a global community, and the political, economic, environmental and social implications of this, and the role of the European Union, the Commonwealth and the United Nations | 15 Born black, born British |

## Other subject links

### English

- Reading – texts from different cultures and traditions.
- Literature – drama, fiction and poetry by major writers from different cultures and traditions.

### Music

- Listening and applying knowledge and understanding – identify the contextual influences that affect the way music is created, performed and heard (for example, intention, use, venue, occasion, development of resources, impact of ICT, the cultural environment and the contribution of individuals).
- Breadth of study – a range of live and recorded music from different times and cultures.

# 1

# African roots

The story of black Caribbean people begins in Africa. Today this continent, the second largest in the world, has 53 independent countries, a total population in excess of 807,419,000, more than 3,000 recognised ethnic groups and over 1,000 separate languages.

Modern political map of Africa

It is said that the history of the African continent is the history of humankind itself, for it is here that the earliest fossils of human ancestors have been found. Recent archaeological and scientific findings support the theory that the beginnings and early evolution of human life began in this continent. Hence Africa is given the name 'cradle of humankind'.

## Ancient African civilisations

Africa was the home of one of the first civilisations to emerge in the ancient world: the old kingdom of Egypt in the fertile Nile valley was established around 3,000 BC and lasted for over 3,000 years. It was the most enduring state in the history of the world. Perhaps because it was also one of the most peaceable, the ancient Egyptians became a highly civilised society with surprisingly advanced scientific knowledge, medicine and technology.

During the period 1,000–500 BC, iron-smelting and metal working as well as sophisticated stone and clay working techniques were developed in various parts of Africa and spread across the continent. These skills, combined with the wealth that came from gold mining, were the foundation of a number of highly civilised kingdoms in West Africa. The introduction of the camel in 100 BC made it possible to cross the desert with goods, so trans-Sahara trade routes were established. The earliest of these kingdoms was Ghana (in a different location to modern Ghana). There, the Islamic city of Timbuktu became a flourishing centre of art, learning and trade.

A view of Timbuktu, 19th-century engraving

Leo Africanus was a sixteenth-century scholar who was commissioned by Pope Leo X to write a detailed survey of Africa. He wrote an account of Timbuktu following a visit, probably made around 1512. This extract is based on a nineteenth-century translation.

> *Yet there is a most stately temple to be seen, the walls whereof are made of stone and lime; and a royal palace also built by a most excellent artist from Granada. Here are many shops of artificers, and merchants, and especially of such as weave linen and cotton cloth. And hither do the Barbary merchants bring cloth of Europe …*
>
> *Here are great store of doctors, judges, priests, and other learned men, that are bountifully maintained at the king's cost and charges. And hither are brought diverse manuscripts or written books out of Barbary, which are sold for more money than any other merchandise. The coin of Tombuto is of gold without any stamp or superscription: but in matters of small value they use certain shells brought hither out of the kingdom of Persia …*
>
> *The inhabitants are people of a gentle and cheerful disposition, and spend a great part of the night in singing and dancing through all the streets of the city.*

Other powerful states emerged, including Mali, Songhai and Benin. On sites in each of these areas, archaeological excavations have revealed the existence of wealthy societies with systematic taxation, well-organised armies, highly developed craftsmanship and flourishing trade.

15th-century Benin bronze carving

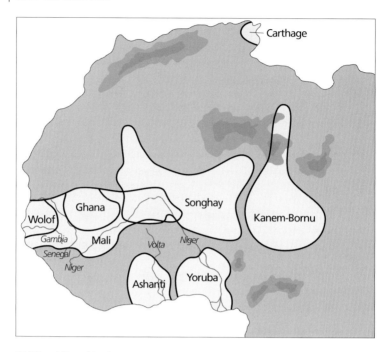

Old West African kingdoms

Map of North and West Africa, engraving, 1522

## Europeans in Africa

Early in the fifteenth century, helped by improvements in navigation and cartography, the Portuguese began to venture along the West African coast. They were seeking to develop trade in gold and other profitable commodities, and by the middle of the century they had established trading posts along the coast as far as Senegal.

John Wesley, the founder of the Methodist church, never visited Africa himself, but in 1774 he published *Thoughts upon Slavery*, in which he examined the life of people in various parts of Africa based on eyewitness accounts.

*We come next to inquire what sort of men they are, of what temper and behaviour, not in our plantations; but in their native country. And here likewise the surest way is to take our account from eye and ear witnesses. Now, those who have lived in the Senegal country observe, it is inhabited by three nations, the Jalofs, Fulis, and Mandingos. The King of the Jalofs has under him several Ministers, who assist in the exercise of justice. The Chief Justice goes in circuit through all his dominions, to hear complaints and determine controversies; and the Viceroy goes with him, to inspect the behaviour of the Alkadi, or Governor, of each village. The Fulis are governed by their chief men, who rule with much moderation. Few of them will drink anything stronger than water, being strict Mahometans. The Government is easy, because the people are of a quiet and good disposition, and so well instructed in what is right, that a man who wrongs another is the abomination of all. They desire no more land than they use, which they cultivate with great care and industry: If any of them are known to be made slaves by the white men, they all join to redeem them. They not only support all that are old, or blind, or lame among themselves, but have frequently supplied the necessities of the Mandingos, when they were distressed by famine.*

*It was of these parts of Guinea that Monsieur Allanson, correspondent of the Royal Academy of Sciences at Paris, from 1749 to 1753, gives the following account, both as to the country and people: – 'Which way soever I turned my eyes, I beheld a perfect image of pure nature: An agreeable solitude, bounded on every side by a charming landscape; the rural situation of cottages in the midst of trees; the ease and quietness of the Negroes, reclined under the shade of the spreading foliage, with the simplicity of their dress and manners: The whole revived in my mind the idea of our first parents, and I seemed to contemplate the world in its primitive state. They are, generally speaking, very good-natured, sociable, and obliging. I was not a little pleased with my very first reception; and it fully convinced me, that there ought to be a considerable abatement made in the accounts we have of the savage character of the Africans.' He adds: 'It is amazing that an illiterate people should reason so pertinently concerning the heavenly bodies. There is no doubt, but that, with proper instruments, they would become excellent astronomers.' …*

*The natives of the kingdom of Benin are eminently civil and courteous: If you make them a present, they endeavour to repay it double; and if they are trusted till the ship returns the next year, they are sure honestly to pay the whole debt.*

## ⊙ Points for reflection

1. From the photographs of African metalwork and Leo Africanus' description, what sort of picture can we get of ancient civilisations in Africa? What were the characteristics of ancient African societies?

2. Improvements in navigation enabled Portuguese explorers to reach Africa by sea. What difference did this make to the relationship of European countries to Africa?

3. From John Wesley's description, what sort of society did the European explorers encounter? How did the Europeans view the African people? How did the African people behave towards the Europeans? What might have been the thoughts and reactions of the Africans on encountering the European visitors?

## ●→ Find out more

What has archaeological and historical research told us about the ancient kingdoms of Mali, Songhai and Benin?

# 2

# Slavery

Slavery is a very ancient practice that has been in existence possibly since humankind first settled in agricultural communities. It is mentioned in both the Bible and the Koran and can be traced back to the ancient civilisations of the Mayans, the Aztecs, the Babylonians and the Egyptians. In most ancient societies, slavery was an established institution and part of the way of life.

A slave can be defined as a person who is owned by another for the purpose of forced, unpaid labour. Many slaves in ancient societies were people who had been taken captive in a war or in a siege on a neighbouring community.

The status and treatment of slaves has varied greatly across and also within different societies. Similarly, the work done by a slave could be anything from labouring in a sugar cane field to being a musician or a teacher. But even for those in privileged positions, slaves' lives were not their own: they were essentially another person's property, and as such could be used or sold as the owner desired.

**Word origins**

**Slave** from the word *slav*. The slavs, a people who inhabited part of eastern Europe, were taken into slavery by Spanish Muslims in the ninth century AD.

**Serve** from the Latin *servire*, meaning 'to serve'. The Roman word for slave was servus (pronounced 'ser-wuss').

## Slavery in ancient civilisations

In ancient Greece, slaves were used for many different types of work, including domestic service, farming, building, mining, policing and fighting. It is thought that slaves in the Greek city-states were reasonably well treated and there were laws to protect them from abuse. Freedom could be bought or be granted for good service.

The Greek philosopher Aristotle proposed a theory that people are either slaves or masters by nature.

> *For a man who is able to belong to another person is by nature a slave (for that is why he belongs to someone else), as is a man who participates in reason only so far as to realise that it exists, but not so far as to have it himself – other animals do not recognise reason, but follow their passions. The way we use slaves is not very different; assistance regarding the necessities of life is provided by both groups, by slaves and by domestic animals. Nature must therefore have intended to make the bodies of free men and of slaves different also; slaves' bodies strong for the services they have to do, those of free men upright and not much use for that kind of work, but instead useful for community life.*
>
> Aristotle (384–322 BC) *Politics*

Similarly, slave labour underpinned the Roman Empire and slaves were an integral part of the fabric of Roman society. There were many different categories of slave and some could be found in highly skilled work or privileged positions. Educated slaves, for example, could become doctors or lawyers.

Slaves in Rome were regarded as the property of their owners and were denied many civil rights. However, evidence suggests they were viewed as

people, rather than as mere objects. Even though cruelty to slaves was undoubtedly practised by some masters, it was not considered acceptable. Thus, slaves were able to keep their own name, to marry and have a family, to speak their own language and worship according to their own religion. It was also possible, in some circumstances, for slaves to gain their freedom.

Fragment of a Roman fresco showing slaves preparing a meal, first century AD

Although there are records of black African slaves in these civilisations, there appears to have been no difference in the status of black and whites slaves, nor did slavery have any racial connotations. Moreover, not all black people living in Mediterranean societies were slaves.

## Slavery in Africa

Long before the arrival of Europeans, slavery was common within many African societies. These slaves were kept mainly for domestic use and not for trade. Neither were Europeans the first people to trade in African slaves. Muslim Arabs from the Middle East raided African communities, capturing both men and women and transporting them to Asia where they were used in agricultural and domestic service. Women were often sold as sex slaves.

By the fourteenth century, black African slaves could be found throughout the Mediterranean lands and even in mainland Europe. They were taken across the trans-Sahara trade routes and sold in Mediterranean ports.

In the fifteenth century, improvements in cartography and navigation enabled Portuguese ships to sail along the west coast of Africa. The main attraction was African gold, which was the basis of the European economy at the time. Among the other commodities they found they could acquire were black slaves. Before long, the Portuguese were shipping human cargo as well.

In 1441, a Portuguese sea captain named Antam Goncalves is recorded as having captured ten Africans near Cape Bojador. This is considered to mark the beginning of the slave trade. The first slave consignment arrived in the Algarve (southern Portugal) in 1444, and just four years later over 1,000 Africans had been deported to mainland Portugal and to the sugar plantations on the West African islands. At first, most of the slaves were captured by the Portuguese themselves, but soon they were being bought from African traders.

It is estimated that a total of 200,000 African slaves were shipped to parts of Europe by the Portuguese and others. But these first diversions into Europe were just the prelude to something on a much larger scale, as black slaves became a vital link in a chain of global trade that would transform the face of three continents.

## Slavery and religion

Not only was slavery an accepted part of life in ancient societies, it was also accepted by the main religions including Judaism, Christianity and Islam.

Although Christianity was eventually to play a part in the abolition of slavery, early Christian communities saw slavery as part of the natural order of existence. In other words, their view was similar to that in the rest of the Middle East at the time. Early Christian communities were less concerned with changing the fabric of society than with the faith and conduct of the individual and the religious community within it. Hence Christianity did influence the way slaves were treated – it was one of the forces that brought in new Roman laws on humane treatment of slaves, for example – but for the most part it did not question the morality of slavery itself.

> *Children, obey your parents in the Lord, for this is right. 'Honour your father and mother' – this is the first commandment with a promise, 'that it may be well with you and that you may live long on the earth.'*
>
> *Slaves, be obedient to those who are your earthly masters, with fear and trembling, in singleness of heart, as to Christ; not in the way of eye service as men-pleasers, but as servants of Christ, doing the will of God from the heart.*
>
> The Bible, Ephesians Chapter 6, The Revised Standard Version

Islam, while accepting slavery as part of the human state of affairs, provided for the humane treatment of slaves. In Islamic law, the freeing of slaves is one of the actions suggested for a believer who does wrong.

> *Allâh will not punish you for what is unintentional in your oaths, but He will punish you for your deliberate oaths; for its expiation (a deliberate oath) feed ten Masâkin (poor persons), on a scale of the average of that with which you feed your own families; or clothe them; or manumit a slave.*
>
> The Qu'rân, An-Nur 2:221

The first Portuguese traders who became involved with African slavery believed that they were justified in their actions because they were converting the Africans to Christianity. But whatever their original intentions, ideas of conversion were soon swept aside by the possibilities of commercial gain.

There were some Christian dissenters who argued that men should not be bought and sold like cattle, but their lone voices were largely unheard.

⊙ **Points for reflection**

1. Aristotle compares slaves with animals. Scholars studying slavery have compared the way societies have used slaves with the way they used animals, suggesting that the domestication of animals has been a model for enslaving people. What arguments could be put forward to support this view? Are there any arguments against it? What is your opinion on it?

2. Christianity and Islam both view human life as created by God and having a special value. How were these religions able to see slavery as an accepted part of society?

●→ **Find out more**

Slavery still exists in some parts of the world. Where and why does it continue? What is life like for the enslaved people and what is being done to oppose the practice?

# 3 | The Caribbean

The Caribbean islands lie in the Caribbean Sea, south-east of North America and north-east of South America. The islands vary in size. Cuba, for example, has an area of 110,860 sq. km (42,792 sq. miles), which is slightly less than the area of England; Antigua has an area of only 442 sq. km (171 sq. miles), and there are hundreds of islands that are smaller still.

## Present-day Caribbean

The islands are spread across thousands of miles and are generally divided into three groups: the Bahamas, the Greater Antilles and the Lesser Antilles. The Bahamas is the name given to the hundreds of smaller islands off the east coast of Florida. The Greater Antilles are generally larger islands and these lie closer to the United States, while the Lesser Antilles are the smaller islands south-east of Puerto Rico. The Lesser Antilles are further divided into the Leeward Islands, the Windward Islands and the Netherlands Antilles.

Today, the inhabitants of these islands are of very diverse ethnic background and include people of African, Native American, and European descent. A variety of languages are spoken across the region, but the four official ones are English, Spanish, French and Dutch. Just as the countries of Europe, for example, have different peoples, languages and culture, so each group of islands, and even individual islands, have their own distinct languages and culture.

Many of the Caribbean islands are in the tropics and have a tropical climate, although this is moderated to some extent by the prevailing north-east trade winds. Local temperatures also vary according to altitude. Rather than having the four seasons of a temperate climate, such as that in Britain, the

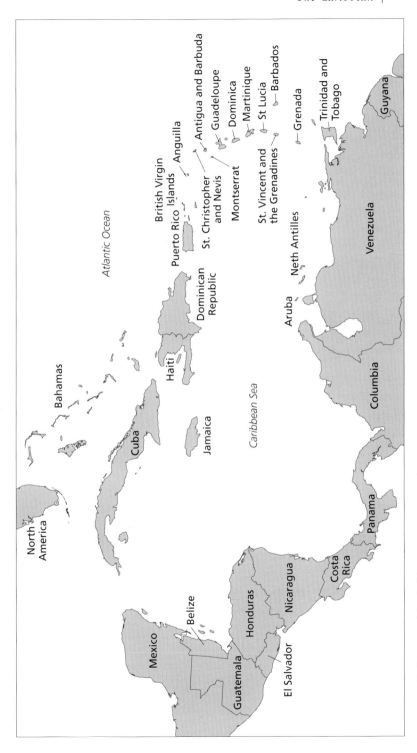

Modern map of the Caribbean

Caribbean climate is characterised by high temperatures throughout the year and a rainy season from May to October. The Bahamas are situated just north of the Tropic of Cancer and experience more temperature variation than the tropical islands.

**Caribbean** from *Carib* – the name of one of the earliest indigenous peoples

**West Indies** the islands were given this name after they were discovered by Christopher Columbus, the fifteenth-century navigator who had been trying to reach India

**Antilles** from the French and Dutch name for the islands

**Jamaica** from *Xamayca*, the Arawak (Native American Indian) name for the island, meaning 'land of wood and water'

## Jamaica

The Atlantic slave trade affected many of the islands of the Caribbean as well as North and Central America, and each region has its own story to tell. The British colonies were mainly in the Caribbean, and the most significant of these was Jamaica. As this book focuses on the particular relationship of Caribbean people with Britain, the historical narrative focuses particularly on the situation and events on Jamaica.

Jamaica

With an area of 10,957 sq. km (4,229 sq. miles) that is, about half the size of Wales, Jamaica is one of the larger islands. Much of the land is mountainous and the highest point is the Blue Mountain Peak at 2,256 m (7,402 ft). The average temperature ranges from 26 to 30 °C, and the rainfall on the island varies widely between 200 cm and up to 760 cm in the Blue Mountains. Like much of the Caribbean, Jamaica is prone to hurricanes, which cause devastation on an annual basis.

## The indigenous people

Before the arrival of Europeans at the end of the fifteenth century, the Caribbean islands were inhabited solely by various groups of Native American Indians. One ethnic group were the Arawaks – American Indians who had originally colonised the islands from north-eastern South America. Arawakian Indians in different parts of the Caribbean acquired different names for themselves, but Taino – the name by which these people introduced themselves to the Spanish explorers – is the term generally used for this group.

The Tainos of the Caribbean were a self-sufficient, highly skilled people who had adapted to life on the islands. They were proficient in agriculture and grew a variety of crops including maize, yams, cotton and tobacco, employing crop rotation to prevent soil erosion. They produced pottery and carving, and could spin and weave; from cotton they wove clothing, hammocks, sailcloth, ropes, carpets and watertight roofs. They were also

Arawak canoe at the entrance of the Columbus Park, Jamaica

skilled boat builders and seafarers. Columbus was said to be impressed with the massive canoes hewn from silk cotton trees, which were as long as 30 m (98.5 ft) and able to hold up to 50 people.

In the Lesser Antilles, the Tainos were driven out by another race called the Carib. The Spanish term for these Native Americans, *Caníbales*, is the root of the English word 'cannibal'. While the Caribs do appear to have been a relatively aggressive people, there is no evidence that they were really cannibals. They may have been given the label simply because they resisted captivity at the hands of the invading Europeans and fought vigorously for their land and their freedom.

## The arrival of Europeans

In 1492, Christopher Columbus and 120 Spanish adventurers arrived in the Caribbean. Columbus had set out believing that he could reach India by sailing westward, hence the name West Indies. His object was to find sources of trade and wealth for Spain. On arrival in the Caribbean, Columbus visited the Bahamas, Cuba and Haiti at the start of what was to be a Spanish invasion of the Caribbean and Central America.

Christopher Columbus, painting by Roldan, 1881

Columbus' logbook records his thoughts on meeting the indigenous people.

*Two o'clock in the morning the land was discovered, at two leagues' distance; they took in sail and remained under the square-sail lying to till day, which was Friday, when they found themselves near a small island, one of the Lucayos, called in the Indian language Guanahani. Presently they descried people, naked, and the Admiral landed in the boat, which was armed, along with Martin Alonzo Pinzon, and Vincent Yanez his brother, captain of the Nina.*

*Arrived on shore, they saw trees very green many streams of water, and diverse sorts of fruits. The Admiral called upon the two Captains, and the rest of the crew who landed, as also to Rodrigo de Escovedo notary of the fleet, and Rodrigo Sanchez, of Segovia, to bear witness that he before all others took possession (as in fact he did) of that island for the King and Queen his sovereigns, making the requisite declarations, which are more at large set down here in writing. Numbers of the people of the island straightway collected together. Here follow the precise words of the Admiral: 'As I saw that they were very friendly to us, and perceived that they could be much more easily converted to our holy faith by gentle means than by force, I presented them with some red caps, and strings of beads to wear upon the neck, and many other trifles of small value, wherewith they were much delighted, and became wonderfully attached to us. Afterwards they came swimming to the boats, bringing parrots, balls of cotton thread, javelins, and many other things which they exchanged for articles we gave them, such as glass beads, and hawk's bells; which trade was carried on with the utmost good will.*

*Weapons they have none, nor are acquainted with them, for I showed them swords which they grasped by the blades, and cut themselves through ignorance. They have no iron, their javelins being without it, and nothing more than sticks, though some have fish-bones or other things at the ends. They are all of a good size and stature, and handsomely formed. I saw some with scars of wounds upon their bodies, and demanded by signs; they answered me in the same way, that there came people from the other islands in the neighbourhood who endeavoured to make prisoners of them, and they defended themselves. I thought then, and still believe, that these were from the continent. It appears to me, that the people are ingenious, and would be good servants and I am of opinion that they would very readily become Christians, as they appear to have no religion.'*

On his second voyage to the Americas in 1493, Columbus landed on Jamaica at Santa Gloria (St Ann's Bay). He took the island by force for the Spanish and named it Santa Jago after Spain's patron saint.

No one really knows the size of the Taino population when Columbus arrived: estimates range from 6,000 to 100,000.

In the early part of the sixteenth century, Jamaica was a Spanish colony. Spain, however, lost some of its interest in the island when it became clear there was no gold to be mined. The Spanish settlers established small farms and used the Tainos as labour. Eventually, the majority of the indigenous people were dispersed. Some were undoubtedly hunted and killed; some were taken captive and used as slaves. Those that remained on the island had poor resistance to the Spanish diseases and many died as a result of infection. By the mid-seventeenth century, Jamaica's indigenous population had been wiped out as a consequence of the Spanish invasion.

---

⊙ **Points for reflection**

1. From the logbook extract, what is Columbus' attitude towards the indigenous people? What are his intentions for them? What assumptions underlie his description?

2. Columbus said of the island people, 'They appear to have no religion.' Is it possible that Columbus had come to the wrong conclusion, and if so, why?

3. Is Spain's subsequent treatment of the Indian people in line with Columbus' initial reactions? What explanation could there be for any apparent change in attitude?

4. The whole indigenous population in Jamaica was wiped out by people from another country and the same happened in other Caribbean islands. What factors made this possible?

---

●→ **Find out more**

---

What of the Tainos' culture survives in the present day, in the Caribbean or elsewhere?

---

# 4

# Conquest and cultivation

At the end of the fifteenth century, the Caribbean islands entered a period of transformation, as wave after wave of European adventurers arrived and laid claim to land. Their interest was in exploiting the local natural resources. They saw rocks that could be mined and land that could be cultivated with valuable crops that could not easily be grown in the temperate climate of western Europe. The most significant of these was sugar.

## Sugar – the sacred reed

For many thousands of years, honey was the only sweetener used. It was not easy to mass produce and so was considered a luxury. Tradition has it that sugar cane was probably first grown in Papua New Guinea about 5,000 years ago, and then taken by sailors and traders to India and other parts of the Far East. In 510 BC, the Persian Emperor Darius invaded India and found that the people sweetened their food with a substance that came from a plant. The Persians called this plant 'the reed which gives honey without bees'.

Sugar cane

When Alexander the Great invaded Persia and North-west India in 326 BC, he also discovered what he called 'the sacred reed'. He brought sugar to the West and soon the Greeks and Romans were importing it as a luxury item.

---

**Word origins**

**Sugar** from the Arabic word *sukkar*

---

For centuries, the cultivation of cane and the method of refining it were kept a closely guarded secret, while the sweet product was sold for a handsome profit. Then, during the seventh century AD, the Arabs invaded Persia, learned the secrets and began production in other regions. With the spread of Islam, knowledge of sugar cultivation reached Spain and North Africa.

In the eleventh century, the Crusaders who had fought in the Holy Land (Palestine in the Middle East) brought samples of sugar back to Europe. The first tasting of sugar recorded in Britain was in 1099. As Western Europe developed trade with the East, sugar was among the imported goods. Henry III is believed to have been the first monarch to enjoy sugar in 1264, but it did not become generally available until the beginning of the fourteenth century. It is recorded that in London in 1319, sugar was being sold at 'two shillings a pound'. This is equivalent to approximately £44 at today's prices, so it remained a luxury that could be afforded only by the nobility and the very rich. In fact, sugar was considered so valuable that it was kept locked in specially adapted tea caddies.

## Cultivation spreads west

In the fifteenth century the Arabs brought sugar cane to Spain and Portugal and both countries sought to find a suitable place where they could grow this valuable crop. Plantations were established on the Canaries, on the Atlantic islands of Madeira and on São Tome, all using African slaves as labour. These plantations flourished, although yields were not as good as those that would later come from the islands of the Caribbean. This was, however, the beginnings of commercial production of sugar for Europe, and the supply further stimulated demand.

Eventually, sugar cane travelled across the Atlantic; Christopher Columbus may even have taken some with him on his second Americas expedition in 1493. The tropical and sub-tropical climate in the West Indies proved ideal growing conditions, and cultivation was far more successful here than anywhere that had been tried previously. Initially, however, not a great deal of sugar was grown on the islands because the Spanish invaders were more interested in the possibilities for commercial gain on mainland South America.

**Sugar consumption in Britain**

| 1700 | 1.8 kg (4 lbs) per capita |
|------|---------------------------|
| 1789 | 5.4 kg (12 lbs) per capita |
| 1809 | 8.2 kg (18 lbs) per capita |

## Spanish colonies and Portuguese slave-traders

When Columbus sailed to the Caribbean and the Americas, there was already an Atlantic slave-powered economy. The Portuguese were taking slaves from West Africa and trading them in the islands along the west side of the Atlantic. Columbus' letter to Catholic Kings in 1446 mentions slaves selling in Cape Verde Islands at 8,000 *maravedis* a head.

However, the Spanish crown kept strict control on the movement of slaves into the Spanish colonies, and a licence was required for any slave transaction. Thus, in the early years of the Spanish settlements, only a very few black African slaves got as far as the Americas. The Spanish were determined to continue using Indian labour, capturing Indians from other islands and taking them to the settlements where labourers were needed. The Indians did not take to the work as the conquistadores had expected and many died from European diseases, such as smallpox, to which they had no resistance.

In 1510, a decree issued by King Ferdinand of Spain allowed 50 African slaves to be taken to Hispaniola (present day Haiti and the Dominican Republic) to work in the gold mines. They proved to be better workers than the Indians: a report to the Spanish king in 1511 stated that the work of one black slave was equal to the work of four Indians.

By this time, the Portuguese had established trading stations along the west coast of Africa and were importing 10,000 African slaves into Portugal every year. Gradually, over the next eight years, the Spanish began to grant more licences (*asiento*) to Portuguese slave traders and so African slaves began to cross the Atlantic.

At first, it was only a trickle. In 1518, Charles, the new king of Spain, granted permission for 4,000 black slaves to be imported into the Spanish colonies. The rights were sold on to Portuguese traders – only they could supply slaves in those numbers – and the first large cargoes of slaves were taken to the Caribbean. These consignments marked the beginning of a trade in humanity on a massive scale that would continue for another two centuries. The floodgates had opened.

During the 1520s, the Spanish realised the sugar-growing potential of the Caribbean islands and began to establish plantations there. However, it was in the Portuguese colony of Brazil in the 1530s and 40s that the sugar industry really took off. The Portuguese had learned about sugar cultivation on Madeira and São Tome, and began to establish small plantations in the Caribbean. To begin with they used American Indians as labour, but soon started to import African slaves. By the 1630s there were 60,000 Africans in Brazil, completely replacing the Indian workforce. The sugar produced stimulated European demand and this in turn encouraged the establishment of more and larger plantations.

## The triangular trade

When Europe began colonising and exploiting the New World, the Spanish were the dominant power, with the Portuguese having control of the trade in African slaves. But other countries were keen to reap their own rewards from this lucrative business. The Dutch and the English were the biggest threat.

The Portuguese were keen to maintain their monopoly of the slave trade, but demand began to exceed what they were able to supply. At first, the competition was rather like piracy, as unlicensed traders from other nations raided West African coastal trading posts, seeking African slaves to take to the Americas.

One of the earliest English slave traders was Sir John Hawkins. In 1562, he set sail for West Africa where he captured 300 Africans, most of whom had already been packed onto one of the Portuguese vessels bound for Cape Verde. He took the slaves to Hispaniola and there traded them for silver, sugar and leather, which he carried back to sell in England. This was the beginning of the system known as 'the triangular trade route'. Encouraged by Queen Elizabeth, the English trade grew and became very profitable.

Sir John Hawkins, 16th-century engraving

Ships on the triangular route would set sail from Britain in July, August or September to avoid arriving in Africa in the rainy season. London, Bristol and Liverpool were the main centres of trade, although other, smaller ports also became involved. Their cargo on the first leg of the journey would consist of firearms, cutlasses, knives, iron goods, brass bowls, cloth and alcohol. They also carried shackles and chains for restraining the enslaved Africans. On arrival in Africa, goods were exchanged for slaves.

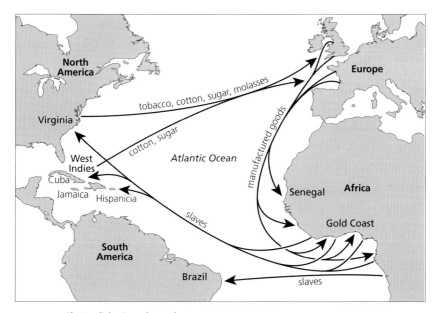

The English triangular trade route

Europeans buying enslaved Africans, 19th-century engraving

The ships then sailed across the Atlantic to the Americas where slaves were sold on to European plantation owners in exchange for sugar, cotton and tobacco, which the ships carried back to England. A similar system was adopted in other European countries, notably France and the Netherlands.

At first, the plantation owners used sugar or rum to purchase new slaves. But when the price of sugar fell in relation to the price of slaves, ships' captains accepted bills of exchange drawn on the accounts of merchants in Europe to whom the sugar was to be delivered. Once the transaction had taken place, a ship would be loaded with tropical produce for the return journey to Europe, thus completing the third leg of the journey.

In 1672 the British Royal African Company was founded to create secure trading posts along the 'British' West African coast. Forts were set up and staffed by British agents who helped to forge links with the African slave dealers. By the eighteenth century many other European countries were involved in the Atlantic slave trade, each with their own national company and a similar system of trading.

**Estimated figures for slave carriage 1701–1800**

| Carrier | Total number of slaves deported |
|---|---|
| English | 2,532,300 |
| Portuguese | 1,796,300 |
| French | 1,180,300 |
| Dutch | 350,900 |
| North America | 194,200 |
| Danish | 73,900 |
| Other (Swedish, Brandenburg) | 5,000 |
| **Total** | **6,132,900** |

From 'The Volume of the Atlantic Slave Trade: A Synthesis',
Paul E. Lovejoy, in *Journal of African History*, 1982

## The British colonies

By the time of Queen Elizabeth's death in 1603, the English had acquired a taste for sugar and tobacco and other tropical produce. So acquiring colonies of their own in which to grow these crops seemed an obvious step. They began to look for other Caribbean islands to exploit, as did the Dutch and the French. The first non-Spanish settlements were shared between these countries, but by the mid-seventeenth century, the Caribbean was the source of much rivalry and conflict as England, France, the Netherlands and Spain all fought to maintain their claims to land and their share of the profits.

In the early part of the seventeenth century, English settlers swarmed across the Atlantic, establishing colonies in Bermuda, Barbados and Antigua. In 1655 they also acquired Jamaica by seizing it from the Spanish.

In the early years of these colonies, many of the workers were indentured labourers: young European men who agreed to work for three to five years in return for their passage, food and housing. However, the cost of these labourers was high and after their indenture they demanded their rights to freedom and land. So the plantation owners turned to the African slave traders.

As the English established their colonies, they also started to become more dominant in the slave trade. Although many European countries were involved, England would eventually become the largest slave-trading nation.

## Ownership of Caribbean Islands 1776–1815

| Country | 1779–1782 | 1782 | 1783 | 1786 | 1795 | 1796 | 1802 | 1804 | 1815 |
|---|---|---|---|---|---|---|---|---|---|
| Antigua | B | | | | | | | | B |
| Bahamas | | Sp | B | | | | | | |
| Barbados | B | | | | | | | | B |
| British Guiana | | | | | | | | | B |
| Cuba | | | | | | | | | Sp |
| Domingue | | | | | | | | Haiti | |
| Dominica | | | B | | | | | | |
| Grenada | | | | | | B | | | |
| Guadeloupe | | | | | | | | | F |
| Haiti | | | | | | | | (Indep.) | |
| Honduras Settlement | Sp | | | B | | | | | |
| Jamaica | B | | | | | | | | B |
| Martinique | | | | | | | | | F |
| Montserrat | | | B | | | | | | |
| Netherlands Antilles | | | | | | | | | F |
| Puerto Rico | | | | | | | | | Sp |
| Santo Domingue | | | | | F | | | | Sp |
| St Kitts-Nevis | | | B | | | | | | |
| St Lucia | | | | | | | | | B |
| St Vincent | | | | | | B | | | |
| Tobago | | | | | | | | | B |
| Trinidad | | | | | | | B | | |

During the seventeenth century and into the eighteenth century, the English colonies expanded and it is estimated that by the 1770s, there were more than 1,800 plantations in the British West Indies. The enterprise had created a set of entrenched social and economic relationships across the Atlantic. The plantation owners needed not only slaves from Africa, but also food, textiles, armaments and other supplies from the rest of the world. These they received in return for the sugar, tobacco and coffee that Europe had come to demand.

In 1787, there was further conflict and Britain lost every island except Jamaica, Barbados and Antigua.

## Sweet success

It was in the British colonies that sugar cultivation and production really became established. Increasing quantities of sugar produced in the British West Indies were supplied to Britain and the rest of Europe. By the eighteenth century, the luxury sweetener had become a mass-market commodity. As well as being used to sweeten coffee and chocolate, sugar was added to tea, which had become a fashionable drink with all social classes. Puddings had become popular and vast quantities of sugar were poured into pies, tarts, steamed puddings, milk puddings and ices. Annual sugar consumption in Britain increased from around 10,000 tons in 1700 to 80,000 tons in 1800 – which would be an average of about 7.3 kg (16 lbs) per person.

## Jamaica

In 1655, a raid led by Admiral William Penn and General Robert Venables, succeeded in gaining control of the Spanish island of Santa Jago. The English ordered the Spanish to surrender all their land, slaves and possessions and leave the island. Most complied, but a small group of Spaniards fled to the mountains and put up resistance. A number of freed black slaves joined them, but some also fought on the side of the English. In 1660 the Spanish resistance was finally defeated and the Spaniards fled. The black slaves who had fought against them were given freedom and land in recognition of their contribution. A number of the Spanish-owned slaves continued to live freely on the island and were known as Maroons (see Chapter 8).

Over the next 100 years, Jamaica was to become established as Britain's most prized colony and was eventually the world's largest exporter of sugar. By 1670 there were approximately 140 plantations, and by 1685 there were at least 690. Towards the end of the eighteenth century, coffee had also become a major export.

**Jamaican sugar export**

| | |
|---|---|
| 1781 | 60,000 tons |
| 1800 | 70,000 tons |
| 1805 | 100,000 tons |

⊙  Points for reflection

1.  What were the main reasons behind European countries' desire to acquire land in the Americas?

2.  What reasons might England and other European countries have had to set up their own slave-trading operations, rather than simply buying slaves from the established Portuguese traders?

3.  What were the differences between indentured labour and slave labour?

●→ Find out more

Over nearly three centuries, millions of Africans were transported across the Atlantic Ocean to provide slave labour in European colonies. Scholars have calculated that it was a terribly expensive operation; importing European convicts, for example, would have been much cheaper. There were also many risks involved. Why did European countries choose to do it? What possible reasons might they have had for importing African slaves?

# 5

# Capture and deportation

From the beginnings of the transatlantic slave trade in the 1520s to its last years at the end of the nineteenth century, an estimated 13 million African people were deported on ships bound for European colonies.

## Sold into slavery

At first, people were taken mainly from Africa's western coast, but later they came from the interior as well. The slave-trading posts stretched from Senegal down to Angola. Each European country had its own preferences about where slaves came from: the French and Spanish bought Yoruba people from Benin, while the British generally took people who were Akan, Ashanti and Fanti from the Gold Coast. The six most badly affected areas each lost more than a million people.

**Origins of African slaves**

| Country | People deported |
|---|---|
| Congo/Angola | 3,000,000 |
| Senegambia, Sierra Leone | 2,000,000 |
| Slave Coast (Dahomey, Adra, Oyo) | 2,000,000 |
| Benin to Calabar | 2,000,000 |
| Gold Coast (Ashanti) | 1,500,000 |
| Mozambique/Madagascar | 1,000,000 |

The plantation owners preferred to take strong young men, but women and children were also enslaved. Cargoes from different regions had different ratios of male and female slaves. Over the whole span of the slave trade, however, men outnumbered women. Children accounted for less than ten per cent of the total, although in the last years of the trade, the supply of children increased to meet a rising demand from the cotton plantations.

Africa in the 18th century, showing areas of slave-trading activity

Venture Smith (1729?–1805) detailed his eyewitness account of being captured as a slave.

> The army of the enemy was large ... After destroying the old prince, they decamped and immediately marched towards the sea ... The enemy had remarkable success in destroying the country wherever they went. For as far as they had penetrated, they laid the habitations waste and captured the people ... All the march I had very hard tasks imposed on me, which I must perform on pain of punishment. I was obliged to carry on my head a large flat stone used for grinding our corn, weighing ... as much as twenty-five pounds; besides victuals, mat and cooking utensils. Though I was pretty large and stout of my age, yet these burdens were very grievous to me, being only six years and a half old.
>
> Venture Smith, *A Narrative of the Life and Adventures of Venture Smith, a Native of Africa, but Resident above Sixty Years in the United States of America*, New London, 1798

## The long march

When the European traders arrived on the coast of Africa, slave trading was already well established. The Islamic slave trade had moved thousands of slaves across the continent long before the transatlantic trade began. The Europeans rarely captured people themselves but established trade with African dealers who could supply slaves in return for goods. When slaves arrived in the hands of European ships' captains, this could be the final link in a complex chain of trading begun many months earlier.

By the time slaves arrived in the coastal trading ports, most had already travelled miles within Africa and could have been sold several times already. They might have been taken as prisoners of war, seized during a raid or simply kidnapped. After being captured inland, they would have been marched across country on foot on a journey that could take anything up to a year. The traders were not concerned with the needs and welfare of these people, and some historians think it possible that as many died on the journey to the ports as on the journey across the Atlantic.

Gang of slaves being marched across Mozambique, 19th-century engraving

## At the coastal trading posts

At the coastal trading centre, the captives were kept chained up in pens called *barracoons*, or in forts that previously had been used for trading gold. Here they were kept, often in atrocious conditions, until handed over for loading onto a slave ship.

Coastal trading ports

The European traders arrived on the West African coast in ships loaded with European goods. Over time they brought goods in ever greater variety and larger quantities as African dealers increased their prices. The cargoes from Europe would have a high value – the equivalent of millions of pounds in today's money. It was a complex system of transactions in which European

Slaves and slave merchants on the west coast of Africa, painted by Francois-Auguste Baird in 1832

goods, such as textiles, firearms and alcohol, were traded for African currency such as shells or gold. This could then be exchanged for slaves.

Ships usually stayed on the African coast for between four and six months, occasionally longer. Some would sail along a stretch of coast, stopping off at several trading centres; others would load all their slaves in one port. Generally, the European traders stayed for as short a time as possible. The longer they stayed, the greater the risk that they and their crew would catch potentially lethal diseases. A delayed departure also meant the slaves had to endure the terrible conditions for even longer. This meant more would sicken and die during the voyage – which would make the crossing more difficult for the traders and reduce their profits.

## Setting sail

Once a ship had acquired its quota of slaves, it loaded supplies for the voyage and then set sail across the Atlantic, assisted by the south-east trade wind.

The slave ships changed very little over the course of 300 years. They were not purpose-built: most were small merchant sailing vessels, rigged for speed. They carried about 300 slaves on average; some were forced to depart with many fewer than their expected quota while others were badly overcrowded.

Slave ships also had a large crew; as well as sailors there were carpenters, cooks and hired guards. There would also be a surgeon whose job it was to advise on the selection of slaves as well as to provide medical treatment on the voyage.

## The Middle Passage

Many of the slaves had already suffered traumatic and physically debilitating experiences prior to boarding the ships. But worse was to come.

Olaudah Equiano (*c.* 1745–1797) was an African slave who was captured and deported on a slave ship at the age of eleven. Eventually he managed to gain his freedom and came to Britain where he became involved in the movement to abolish the slave trade, an involvement that led to him writing and publishing *The Interesting Narrative of the Life of Olaudah Equiano, or Gustavus Vassa the African* (1789), a strongly abolitionist autobiography. The book became a best-seller and, as well as furthering the anti-slavery cause, made Equiano a rich man.

Here he writes about his experience of boarding a slave ship.

*When I looked round the ship too, and saw a large furnace of copper boiling, and a multitude of black people of every description chained together, every one of their countenances expressing dejection and sorrow, I no longer doubted of my fate, and, quite overpowered with horror and anguish, I fell motionless on the deck and fainted ...*

*I was soon put down under the decks, and there I received such a salutation in my nostrils as I had never experienced in my life; so that, with the loathsomeness of the stench, and crying together, I became so sick and low that I was not able to eat, nor had I the least desire to taste anything. I now wished for the last friend, Death, to relieve me; but soon, to my grief, two of the white men offered me eatables; and, on my refusing to eat, one of them held me fast by the hands, and laid me across, I think, the windlass, and tied my feet, while the other flogged me severely ...*

*... the white people looked and acted, as I thought, in so savage a manner; for I had never seen among any people such instances of brutal cruelty; and this not only shewn towards us blacks, but also to some of the whites themselves. One white man in particular I saw, when we were permitted to be on deck, flogged so unmercifully with a large rope near the foremast, that he died in consequence of it; and they tossed him over the side as they would have done a brute. This made me fear these people the more; and I expected nothing less than to be treated in the same manner.*

From *The Interesting Narrative of the Life of Olaudah Equiano,
or Gustavus Vassa the African,* 1789

For this voyage across the Atlantic, known as 'the Middle Passage', the crew fitted the holds of the ships with wooden slatted shelving; this allowed the ships to be filled with as many slaves as possible. The captives – all numbered rather than named – were packed below deck into these confined spaces. Men, women and children were in separate compartments. (There is some evidence to suggest that women were segregated, purely to allow sexual exploitation by the crew.) There was little light or ventilation and poor sanitation. Many were seasick. Lavatories were either a communal bucket or a hole over the sea, but overcrowding made it impossible for some people to reach them. The human cargo was fed regularly – twice a day on British ships – and anyone refusing to eat was force-fed. Some ships carried special instruments for this purpose.

The hold of a slave ship, engraving, 1853

In these conditions, the filth and the stench became overpowering and rat infestation was common. Sickness was rife and many people died from diseases. Dysentery, which was known as 'the bloody flux', accounted for many of the deaths.

Alexander Falconbridge, a surgeon on board a slave ship, described the appalling conditions.

*The deck, that is the floor of their rooms, was so covered with the blood and mucus which had proceeded from them in consequence of the flux that it resembled a slaughter-house. It is not in the power of the human imagination to picture itself a situation more dreadful or disgusting.*

From *An Account of the Slave Trade on the Coast of Africa*,
Alexander Falconbridge, 1788

The crew were supposed to take people in groups out onto the deck to exercise, but often a combination of crew shortage and bad weather meant that people were kept imprisoned below deck for days or even weeks on end. When they were taken out on deck, they were often forced to jump up and down or dance to entertain the crew. Those who did not oblige were whipped or beaten.

## The cost in human lives

Many slaves became severely depressed or overcome with fear and some tried to commit suicide, by starving, suffocating or hanging themselves.

Sailors throwing slaves overboard, from Torrey's
*American Slave Trade*, 1822

When slaves died, they were thrown overboard. Others threw themselves overboard in desperation.

The slaves were not supposed to be kept in chains once stowed below the decks. But evidence suggests that this rule was not always observed.

Dr Thomas Trotter, a doctor who worked on the *Brookes*, made a statement to a House of Commons committee in 1790. He was asked if the slaves had enough room to turn.

*No. The slaves that are out of irons are locked 'spoonways' and locked to one another. It is the duty of the first mate to see them stowed in this manner every morning; those which do not get quickly into their places are compelled by the cat (whip) and, such was the situation when stowed in this manner, and when the ship had much motion at sea, they were often miserably bruised against the deck or against each other. I have seen their breasts heaving and observed them draw their breath, with all those laborious and anxious efforts for life which we observe in expiring animals subjected by experiment to bad air of various kinds.*

Set of iron ankle shackles

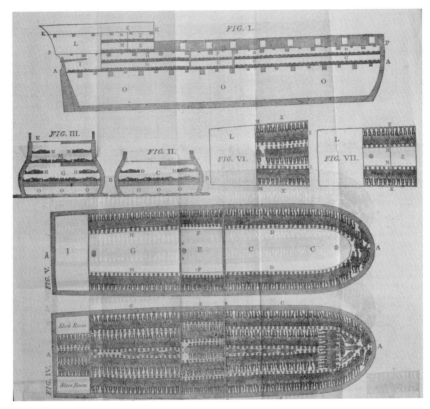

Diagram of the slave ship *Brookes* of Liverpool, wood engraving, 1791

The *Brookes*, a ship that was supposed to take a maximum of 450 people, had carried over 600 slaves from Africa to the Americas, on a voyage that had lasted over eight weeks. Some 60 slaves died and many remained crippled as a result of the conditions.

In fact, research has shown that the worst effect of overcrowding on a ship was not disease, as might be expected – an epidemic would spread as quickly through less crowded decks. There was greater threat from malnutrition and dehydration, simply because more slaves meant less room for supplies

Deaths also resulted from slave rebellions, which occurred on approximately one in nine voyages. Usually these were quickly and brutally put down and dire punishments meted out. There are a few accounts of successful slave revolts, but within a total of 54,000 voyages made over three centuries, their number hardly registers.

Back in Britain, lengthy court cases ensued over deaths on British slave ships. The cases, however, were not murder trials, but disputes over whether insurance companies were liable to pay for the loss of cargo. The most infamous case was that of the ship *Zong*, brought to court in 1783. The ship's captain had calculated that there was not enough water on board to last the voyage and had thrown 133 slaves overboard, in the interests of conserving water supplies. He had believed that the loss would be compensated by the ship's insurance company. The insurers, however, refused to pay out for the jettisoned slaves. While the case was being heard, the abolitionist Granville Sharp wanted to bring a criminal prosecution for murder. At this, John Lee, the Admiralty's Solicitor General, argued that such a thing would be 'madness'. He stated that, 'This is a case of chattels or goods. It is really so: it is the case of throwing over goods; for to this purpose and the purpose of the insurance, they are goods and property'.

The human statistics for the slave trade will never be calculated exactly, but historians estimate that approximately 13 per cent of all Africans who boarded the slave ships died before reaching their destination. This means that about one and a half million people lost their lives in transit. Mortality was highest on the longest journeys. On one protracted and disastrous voyage made by the *George* in 1717, a cargo of 594 slaves was reduced to under a hundred as 496 died.

## Landfall

The duration of voyages was quite variable, but most took between six and eight weeks. For those who had survived, the ordeal of the Middle Passage was over, but they now faced an uncertain future as captives in a strange land – with no hope of return.

---

Olaudah Equiano told of his experience on arriving at the port in Barbados.

> *At last, we came in sight of the island of Barbados, at which the whites on board gave a great shout, and made many signs of joy to us. We did not know what to think of this; but as the vessel drew nearer, we plainly saw the harbour, and other ships of different kinds and sizes, and we soon anchored amongst them, off Bridgetown.*

> *Many merchants and planters now came on board, though it was in the evening. They put us in separate parcels, and examined us attentively. They also made us jump, and pointed to the land, signifying we were to go there. We thought by this, we should be eaten by these ugly men, as they appeared to us; and, when soon after we were all put down under the deck again, there was much dread and trembling among us, and nothing*

---

> *but bitter cries to be heard all the night from these apprehensions,*
> *insomuch, that at last the white people got some old slaves from the land*
> *to pacify us. They told us we were not to be eaten, but to work, and were*
> *soon to go on land, where we should see many of our country people. This*
> *report eased us much. And sure enough, soon after we were landed, there*
> *came to us Africans of all languages.*
>
> From *The Interesting Narrative of the Life of Olaudah Equiano,*
> *or Gustavus Vassa the African,* 1789

When the slave ship finally reached its destination in the Americas or the Caribbean, the slaves were unloaded and herded into a holding pen, camp or warehouse. Here they would be washed, fed and prepared for sale. The majority were inevitably in very poor health – both physically and mentally – but the ship captains would do their best to make them look presentable in order to obtain the highest possible prices. Their skin would be oiled to make them look healthy and men were shaved. Sometimes, slaves were painted by others from their own region of Africa, to make them look more attractive. Nevertheless, conditions in many of these warehouses were hot and overcrowded, so there was still no escape from the sickness and death that had been rife in the hold of the ship.

Amédée-François Frézier, a French engineer who travelled to Brazil in the early eighteenth century, wrote about the slaves in the trading port of Bahia.

> *There are shops full of these wretches, who are entirely naked and bought*
> *like cattle. I cannot think how they can combine this barbarity with the*
> *sayings of religion, which give [the slaves] the same soul as whites.*
>
> Amédée-François Frézier, *Voyage to the South Sea,* 1717

## Africans for sale

Some slaves would have been reserved in advance by plantation owners, and these were simply handed over. Others were sold at auctions where they were made to stand on an auction block while potential buyers inspected them. Another method was the 'scramble' where a group of slaves were put up for sale at a fixed price per head. Buyers would rush in and grab the ones they wanted, creating a noisy and terrifying scene. Slaves were also sold by being hawked from house to house.

Purchasers often had a clear idea of what they were looking for. One plantation owner, Thomas Thistlewood, was known to look for those who were in a 'moderate' condition, because they were 'commonly hardier', and no one older than 16 or 18 years of age. Inevitably, the strongest, healthiest slaves were sold quickly and at higher prices; the old and the sick, called 'refuse slaves', might linger for weeks or even months.

Families of slaves were sometimes kept together when they were sold, but often they separated. Children might be taken from their parents, never to see them again.

The cost of a slave depended on their age and condition. In general, prices rose over the duration of the slave trade. Thomas Thistlewood is recorded as having paid Mr John Hutt £112 for two men and £200 for one boy and three girls on 7 December 1761.

Notice advertising sale of newly arrived Africans

## Branded

Slaves were branded with a hot iron to show whom they belonged to. Slaves could be branded on any part of their body, including their face. This practice began to die away during the 1720s but was still used in cases of slaves who persistently ran away.

Branding iron, probably 19th century

Branding a slave, 19th-century engraving

⊙ **Points for reflection**

1. In the description written by Venture Smith, who are the people described as 'the enemy' likely to be? Who was 'the old prince' and why would he have been destroyed?

2. In Dr Trotter's account, what is meant by 'locked spoonways'? What else is revealed by his account of conditions on board the ship? Is the account likely to be trustworthy – and why, or why not?

3. What similarities and differences are there between Olaudah Equiano's account of conditions on board and Dr Trotter's?

4. In the Zong case, what was the main argument for not conducting a murder trial? What factors could have made it possible for the authorities to accept such an argument?

5. What were the main methods of selling slaves in the colonies? What do they suggest about the way the deported Africans were viewed by the slave merchants and purchasers?

●→ **Find out more**

Olaudah Equiano is one of a few Africans who wrote from first-hand experience of being deported as a slave. From his and/or other accounts, find out more about what it was like being on board ship. What effects would the experiences of the voyage be likely to have on a person who survived?

# 6

# Life on the plantations

After being taken across the Atlantic by European traders, African slaves were sold on to plantation owners who needed more labour. Frequently the new arrivals were in no fit state to work, being sick and distressed as a result of the horrific conditions on the slave ship. However, in the eyes of the plantation owner, work was the only purpose in these people's lives, so now they were trapped in a life of hardship and oppression, with no hope of ever returning home. Some sick slaves were given a period of easier work in order to recuperate; others were given no respite. It is estimated that up to one-third of the deported Africans died within the first three years.

In the early days of the plantations, slave owners on the Caribbean islands had no restraints placed upon them. Slaves were considered to be possessions and could therefore be used in whatever way the owner decided. As a symbol of ownership, the planters gave the recent arrivals new names.

Slave laws were introduced, but these protected the rights of owners, not those of the slaves, and helped to institutionalise slavery. In effect, they gave legal backing to the unjust physical punishment inflicted on the enslaved Africans. Slaves could be bought, sold, whipped, mutilated, tortured and even killed on the whim of their master, with no hope of redress. One law passed in Barbados in 1688 meant that anyone who stole a shilling could be sentenced to death. For stealing or destroying goods, the offender was whipped in public, for up to 40 lashes. If the offence was committed again, their nose was slit and their forehead branded with an iron. If it happened a third time, the offender would die.

Common beliefs among slave owners, compiled from records in 1764.

- *Your slave is your property.*
- *You can kill your slave.*
- *You can do whatever you want to your slave.*
- *You must destroy your slaves' culture.*
- *Slaves cannot marry.*
- *Slaves cannot learn to read and write.*
- *Slaves cannot become Christians.*
- *Slaves will be severely punished, unto death, if they do anything their master does not like.*
- *Slaves can not possess property.*
- *Slaves cannot sell sugar or anything else.*
- *Slaves must be locked up at night.*
- *Slaves must wear a ball and chain.*
- *If you are black you are deemed to be a slave.*
- *Slaves will work from sun up to sun down.*
- *A slave's child belongs to the master.*
- *Slaves cannot meet together.*
- *Free slaves must wear a badge with a blue cross on their right shoulder at all times.*
- *Free slaves must carry a certificate at all times.*
- *A free slave cannot work next to an ordinary slave.*

## Living conditions

On the plantations, slaves were housed in rows of small, dark, single-roomed huts. Usually overcrowded and lacking in sanitation, these poor dwellings stood in stark contrast to the large and luxurious plantation owner's house.

*Wooden floors were an unknown luxury. In a single room were huddled, like cattle, ten or a dozen persons, men, women, and children. We had neither bedsteads, nor furniture of any description. Our beds were collections of straw and old rags, thrown down in the corners and boxed in with boards; a single blanket the only covering.*

From *The Life of Josiah Henson* (1849), the autobiography of a slave

Slave accommodation, Jamaica

The slaves' diet was poor and monotonous. The staple foods were cornmeal imported from America, beans from England and saltfish from Newfoundland. They might occasionally be given meat, but it would be of poor quality. Some slaves were given a small patch of land on which to grow vegetables. There were times when food did not arrive on the islands because of fighting on the seas. Between 1780 and 1787, conflict at sea was the cause of food shortages that resulted in 15,000 slaves dying of starvation.

An inadequate diet, overcrowding and lack of sanitation led inevitably to a lot of illness. Doctors often refused to tend patients with contagious diseases and many slaves died as a result.

One plantation owner, Thomas Thistlewood, wrote in his diary about the activities on the plantation. From 1750 until his death in 1786, he kept a record of the sugar planting, slave breeding and maintenance, slave clothing, slave demography, slave discipline, slave feeding, slave livestock, slave medicine, and slave rebellions. On Wednesday, 11 March, Thistlewood set out the occupations of the slaves in greater detail than usual. There were many absent from work.

> *Employed cutting canes as before, 10 cutters in the field, 3 carts and the canoe employed.*
>
> *Old Tom and Ambo distilling low wines. Little Mimber, Yabba, Teresa, Jenny, Chrishea, Old Catalina and Ellin all sick at home. London and Frank sick at Salt River, besides Hagar, Mary, Silvia, Rose, Sibbe, Achilles, Titus, Hannibal.*
>
> *Also, Celia at the hogstyes disabled, Basheba at Town lying. Dickson and Plymouth stokers.*
>
> *Quacoo, boatswain of the mill.*

> *Quasheba, feeder.*
> *Old Sibyl, turner.*
> *Hanah and Violet, trash carriers.*
> *Mirtilla and Lucy, cane carriers.*
> *3 hands in the canoe.*
> *6 hands with the carts.*
> *4 watchmen, 3 watchwomen.*
> *Abraham looks after cattle.*
> *Phibbah, Dido, Susanah and Nague about the house.*
> *Cruddon, Joe, Coffee, &c. &c. drive the mules.*
> *Nimini clear the gutters, &c. &c.*
> *Rest tying cane tops, and cutting cane.*

## Work

A slave's working day stretched from dawn to dusk. Sugar cultivation was strenuous and unrelenting work owing to the nature of the crop, and in the hot temperatures it was exhausting. To plant the sugar cane, deep holes had to be dug. Manure was used as a fertiliser and slaves had to carry it to the site in baskets balanced on their heads. One basket could weigh up to 36 kg (80 lbs). When the crop was finally harvested, it took 20 tons of cane to produce one ton of sugar. During the harvest, slaves could be expected to work around the clock.

Slaves working in a sugar cane field, Jamaica, 1840s

The strongest slaves were preferred for this particularly hard form of labour, but women (even when pregnant) and children as young as six could be found working in the fields. Weaker slaves would do jobs such as clearing away rubbish. Slaves in the fields worked as gangs, and if the work was not up to standard they would all receive punishment.

Slaves were also used for the more skilled work of distillation. This was a complex process, which today is done by machine. On larger plantations, some slaves worked as house servants.

Over time, slaves moved into more areas of work, becoming builders, carpenters, craftsmen, coach drivers and stockmen. They were also used as sailors on the vessels that traded around the Caribbean and North America. Some went back onto the transatlantic ships as interpreters and domestic servants. Generally, it was the male slaves who had the opportunity to undertake a wider variety of work; women on the whole were limited to working in the field or in the master's house. Both situations presented another set of problems for the women, as will be discussed later in this chapter.

## Discipline

When new slaves arrived on a plantation, the owner would consider it their first task to 'break them in'. In other words, they wanted to ensure that whatever the slaves' mental or physical condition, they would comply with all the demands put upon them and submit to the regime of unrelenting toil.

Slaves were made to keep working by threats, blows and beatings. It was a system maintained by violence. On larger plantations, slave gangs were over-seen by slave drivers, who would whip anyone whom they considered was not working properly.

Persecution and torture were a part of everyday life. Errors, lateness and lack of attention were all routinely punished. Even small mistakes were not to be tolerated: one female slave who dropped a plate had her ear nailed to a tree by her master. Slaves could also be punished simply for using their own initiative. Owners did not want slaves to think for themselves or to show feelings or emotion.

*One day a heavy squall of wind and rain came on suddenly, and my mistress sent me round the corner of the house to empty a large earthen jar. The jar was already cracked with an old deep crack that divided it in the middle, and in turning it upside down to empty it, it parted in my hand. I could not help the accident, but I was dreadfully frightened, looking forward to a severe punishment. I ran crying to my mistress, 'O mistress, the jar has come in two.' 'You have broken it, have you?' she replied; 'come directly here to me.' I came trembling: she stripped and flogged me long and severely with the cow-skin; as long as she had strength to use the lash, for she did not give over till she was quite tired. – When my master came home at night, she told him of my fault; and oh, frightful! how he fell a swearing. After abusing me with every ill name he could think of, (too, too bad to speak in England,) and giving me several heavy blows with his hand, he said, 'I shall come home to-morrow morning at twelve, on purpose to give you a round hundred.' He kept his word – Oh sad for me! I cannot easily forget it. He tied me up upon a ladder, and gave me a hundred lashes with his own hand, and master Benjy stood by to count them for him. When he had licked me for some time he sat down to take breath; then after resting, he beat me again and again, until he was quite wearied, and so hot (for the weather was very sultry), that he sank back in his chair, almost like to faint …*

From F. Westley and A. H. Davis,
*The History of Mary Prince, a West Indian Slave (related by herself),* 1831

Public whipping of a slave, engraving, 1835

Punishment could take various forms; whipping or flogging was the most common. A whipping could be anything from 100 to 150 lashes with a thick leather cart-whip that tore open the flesh. Ebony bushes were also used and these, too, lacerated the skin. Plantation owners would claim with pride that they treated all slaves equally – by which they meant that men and women were given the same punishments.

> *The general system of floggings is to give them a certain number of stripes with a long whip, which inflicts a dreadful laceration, or a dreadful contusion; and then they follow up that by a severe flogging with ebony switches, the ebony being a very strong wirey plant, with small leaves, like myrtle leaf, and under every leaf a very sharp tough thorn, and then after that they rub them with brine.*
>
> From Richard B. Sheridan, *Doctors and Slaves, A Medical and Demographic History of Slavery in the British West Indies, 1680–1834*, Cambridge,1985
>
> *A thong of hard twisted hide, known by this name in the Caribbean in his hand. I heard immediately after, the cracking of the thong, and the house rang to the shrieks of poor Hetty, who kept crying out, 'Oh, Massa! Massa! me dead. Massa! have mercy upon me – don't kill me outright.'*
>
> From F. Westley and A. H. Davies,
> *The History of Mary Prince, a West Indian Slave (related by herself)*, 1831

The treadmill was also used for both men and women alike. It was like a large wooden wheel with steps on which the slaves had to keep walking, their arms tied over their heads. An overseer would whip them using a 'cat-o-nine-tails', to ensure they kept going.

Slaves suffered all kinds of brutal and unjust punishments, and some even died as a result. As slaves, however, they had no rights and no way of appealing for justice, and the slave owners were not considered guilty. Furthermore, plantation owners were quite prepared to kill a troublesome slave as a lesson to the others – and could do so with impunity.

There were a few owners who sought to use more humane methods for controlling their workforce. Matthew Gregory Lewis is one owner recorded as having shown kindness to slaves. Rather than whip his slaves, he would cajole them, threatening that if they did not get on with their work he would sell up and leave. His slaves were reluctant to work for someone else who might not be so lenient, so they tended to comply. Although his approach appeared to be successful, other slave owners disapproved.

Slaves being punished on a treadmill, 19th-century engraving

> *No man could succeed in the planting line but one whose heart was hard and adamant; he must have no pity for the Negro ...*
>
> Benjamin M'Mahon, a bookkeeper who worked in Jamaica for 18 years and on 24 different plantations

Towards the end of slavery there was some let up in the violence. Planters realised that extreme and indiscriminate punishments produced a greater risk of slave revolt and tempered their discipline.

## Women and children

> *Scarce clothing because of poverty, bending over to work or lifting one's dress to keep it clean ... were seen by the slave holder in sexual terms.*
>
> Henry Bibb, an enslaved African

Female slaves had a very difficult time on the plantations. Not only did they have to work and care for their families, but also frequently had to fend off the unwanted attentions of the owner and other men running the plantation. Many owners would see nothing wrong in using the slave women to satisfy themselves, at any time of day or night. The wives of the plantation owners resented this arrangement and would treat the slave women badly, particularly the ones whom their husband had abused. They would even torture them, using devices such as thumbscrews. The sons of planters also abused the black servant girls on the plantation, just as their fathers had before them.

In his diary, the plantation manager Thomas Thistlewood reveals something of the nature of his relationship with his slaves and, in particular, his fascination with the women. He writes about not being able to contain his sexual urges and abusing the female slaves wherever and whenever he liked, even in front of other people. Thistlewood's writing, although using a form of Latin almost as a code, shows a curious lack of any sense of shame over his behaviour.

> … *past 10 a.m.* Cum[1] *Flora, a Congo,* Super[2] Terram[3] *among the canes, above the wall head, right hand of the river, toward the Negro ground. She been for water cress. Gave her 4 bits.*
>
> *About 2 a.m.* Cum *Negroe\* girl,* super *floor, at north bed foot, in the east parlour. \*unknown.*
>
> *1 with, 2 on, 3 the ground*
>
> From Thomas Thistlewood's diary, entries for Tuesday, 10 September

From the age of about 13, women were encouraged to have as many children as possible, purely to provide more workers for the estate. The death rate among slaves was high, and this practice – which owners referred to as 'breeding' – helped them to avoid the expense of having to buy in more. For the plantation owners who abused slave women, any resulting births were a further benefit. Any children in excess of what the plantation required could be sold for profit. As black slaves were not considered to have the same kinds of feelings as white people, owners had no compunction in selling children and splitting up families.

The separation of mother and child, 19th-century engraving from *Uncle Tom's Cabin* by Harriet Beecher Stowe

Mary Prince was a girl born to a slave family in Bermuda. With her first owner, she had a happy carefree life as a child with her family. She then experienced the harsh realities of slavery when the kind owner died. The new owner sold Mary's family and they were separated. This extract is from an account of her conversation with the daughter of the household.

*'Oh, Mary! my father is going to sell you all to raise money to marry that wicked woman. You are my slaves, and he has no right to sell you; but it is all to please her.' She then told me that my mother was living with her father's sister at a house close by, and I went there to see her. It was a sorrowful meeting; and we lamented with a great and sore crying our unfortunate situation … 'Here comes one of my poor picaninnies!' she said, the moment I came in, 'one of the poor slave-brood who are to be sold to-morrow …'*

Mary's mother was said to be inconsolable at losing her children.

Pregnant women had to continue working right up to the onset of labour. After the birth they would be given just one month to rest. Because of the terrible conditions, however, many babies died soon after birth and so it was common practice not to register a child until the age of four weeks. Mothers were prevented from breastfeeding their children after twelve months so that they could become pregnant again.

It was not considered important to build schools or universities on the islands. Most children in white families were sent back to Britain for schooling, and education for black people was prohibited. In the 1670s about 300 sons of Caribbean planters went to school in England every year and by the 1770s up to three-quarters of planters' sons were sent back. It was not until the 1830s that schools were built across the English-speaking colonies.

## Resistance

Slaves did not endure their oppression without resistance, and it took various forms. At one end of the scale, there was a continual undercurrent of defiance: slaves worked more slowly, pretended to be ignorant, were deliberately careless and gave vent to their feelings in veiled insults. More dangerously, some would steal, damage or destroy their owners' property when they had opportunity. In doing so, they always risked extreme punishments or even death. At the other end of the scale, there were occasional slave revolts, or attempted revolts. Unsuccessful rebellion inevitably resulted in grim and bloody penalties. Following a failed uprising in Jamaican in 1760, the leader was decapitated and his head displayed on a pole.

Although plantation owners lived in almost constant fear of violent outbreaks, there were surprisingly few successful rebellions. The notable exception is the slave revolt in the French colony of St Domingue (Haiti). The Revolution in France had promoted the ideals of liberty, equality and fraternity, and ripples of unrest spread to the French colonies. In St Domingue, slave uprisings escalated into a bloody conflict in which the French plantocracy was eventually overthrown. Haiti became the first independent black republic under the leadership of a former slave, Toussaint L'Ouverture.

## Reaching for freedom

Some slaves tried to gain their freedom by running away. They risked being caught and often they were hunted down on horseback with bloodhounds. Other slaves would accompany the hunt and sometimes used this opportunity to run away themselves.

A recaptured runaway would usually be fitted with iron shackles to prevent future escapes and to serve as warning to other slaves. One type of shackle commonly used was a yoke that went around the neck with three long spikes projecting from the sides. This heavy and cumbersome collar made it impossible for the wearer to lie down to sleep. Persistent runaways could have a limb amputated.

Slaves with iron collars, 1835

Occasionally slaves were freed legally by their owners, an act known as 'manumission'. Others were simply released or abandoned when they became too old to work. Some slaves inherited items in their planters' will.

Though legally at liberty, freed black slaves' lives were still controlled by prejudice. They would be marginalised in society and were often only allowed to work as trades people or domestic servants. Discrimination and racism was endemic in Caribbean slave society.

---

### ⊙ Points for reflection

1. From the account and extracts, what experiences were common to slaves on all plantations? What aspects of life could differ, depending on the plantation and the owner?

2. Many of the British plantation owners had grown up in the Church of England and so were familiar with Christian teachings about loving their neighbour and treating others the way they would want to be treated. How could it have been possible for them to treat the African slaves in the way they did, given their religious background?

3. How did the enslavement of Africans on the plantations affect the European view of African people?

4. What would be the short- and long-term effects of splitting up slave families?

5. What might be the difference in experience and attitude between someone who had been deported from Africa and someone born to a slave family in the Caribbean?

6. Although there were a few major slave revolts, there were not as many as might be expected. What do you think might be the reasons for this?

---

### ●→ Find out more

---

Did treatment of slaves in the colonies change over the years, and if so, how and for what reasons? What effect, if any, did changes have on the experience of the slaves?

---

# 7

# Slave communities
# and culture

Such was the slave traders' view of African people that they did not believe family relationships or ties would be of any significance to slaves. Thus, African men, women and children were captured, sold, deported and resold without a thought to their loss of kin.

## Family life

Despite the damage that slavery inflicted on families, African slaves managed to create family groups and structures that were a source of comfort and support. Children born into slavery learned from other family members how to cope in a hostile world. These families were not necessarily built on the western nuclear family model. Moreover, slaves might marry slaves from other plantations, so that the family was only united at weekends and holidays. Nevertheless, these family groups were the foundation of slave communities and, in some places, slave villages. Each community or village developed its own culture and identity.

To begin with, many groups consisted of people with common African nationality and culture. Where possible, slaves liked to be with people from their own African country or region. In their free time they would gather in national or ethnic groups. But in colonial societies, people of all African races and nationalities were thrown together, and the slave society that developed was shaped by many different cultural influences – including that of the European colonists.

Nevertheless, African culture and tradition remained strong. Each fresh delivery of slaves from Africa brought tales of their homeland – and also of the horrific sea crossing. These fresh reminiscences helped the slave society

Group of slaves outside a cabin, date unknown

to keep its cultural memories of Africa alive and ensured that the trauma of the slave ships was not forgotten.

Within the family, traditional skills such as cooking, hair-braiding, wood-carving and the use of herbal remedies were passed on from one generation to the next, often by the women. Traditional African tales were told in family gatherings and also by storytellers who travelled around the plantations. The stories were invariably tales of the weak and the down-trodden overcoming the powerful by shrewdness and cunning. They enabled the slaves to laugh at the unsuspecting plantation owners and at life itself. One very popular collection of stories was about a spider called Anansi.

> *Once upon a time Anansi was living in a very hard country. A law was passed stopping anyone from talking to anybody else or the person would fall down and die. Anansi was always thinking about his stomach so he decided he was going to benefit out of this and so placed himself in a position where passers by would have to talk to him. He got together a hoe, a pick-axe and a machete and started knocking a large rock by the side of a road.*
>
> *Bang! Bang! Bang!*
>
> *'Morning, brother Anansi' said pig.*
>
> *'Morning, brother pig'*
>
> *'What are you doing?' asked brother pig.*

Anansi replied, 'The government has passed a law that said a famine is coming so everybody must work the ground, so I'm doing what I can.'

While Anansi carried on banging the rock, pig walked on a little way shaking his head, 'Poor Anansi, other people would work on good ground but look at Anansi working on a rock.' Immediately, pig dropped to the ground, dead.

Anansi turned around and picked him up, 'That's the way to do it.' Anansi took pig home for dinner.

The next day he repeated the same thing at the side of the road. Cow came by.

Bang! Bang! Bang!

'Morning, brother Anansi' said cow.

'Morning, brother cow'

'What are you doing?' asked brother cow.

Anansi replied, 'The government has passed a law that said a famine is coming so everybody must work the ground, so I'm doing what I can.'

While Anansi carried on banging the rock, cow walked on by and said, 'Poor Anansi, other people would work on good ground but look at Anansi working on a rock.' Cow dropped to the ground, dead.

Anansi turned around and picked him up, 'That's the way to do it.' Anansi took cow home and ate him.

This also happened to horse and goat.

A few days later, Anansi was at his usual place. Bang! Bang! Bang!

Duck came up and said 'Morning, brother Anansi.'

'Morning, brother duck'

'What are you doing?' asked brother duck.

Anansi replied, 'The government has passed a law that said a famine is coming so everybody must work the ground, so I'm doing what I can. What is all the news in your area?'

'Nothing strange, but last night I had a dream that I've been single for too long, so I'm going to go and find myself someone,' said duck passing by.

Anansi said to himself, 'Oh good people get married and duck wants to get married too!' Just then, Anansi fell down, dead. Duck turned around and picked him up, swallowed him and said, 'That's the way to do it.'

## Music

Music-making and dancing were an integral part of African culture and of slave society. In the fields and the sugar distilleries, slaves sang as they worked. Music was also a way of socialising and having fun as well as being an element in many religious ceremonies.

Using a wide variety of home-made instruments, from drums and shakers to stringed instruments, slaves in every colony made music and danced at every opportunity. The style of African dancing was very different from anything the white people on the island were accustomed to. Whereas Europeans had very formal dances such as the waltz and the quadrille, African dances were much more energetic, with dancers improvising and moving around freely. Spectators and participants would form a circle, then the dancers would move into the centre, moving their hips rhythmically to the beat of the drums.

Good dancers were held in high regard by slave communities and many women were given money if they danced well. Slave owners were known to enjoy watching the dancers, especially the seductive movements of the women, but they also felt uncomfortable with it. Edward Long, a writer and planter who lived on the island of Jamaica for 12 years, commented on the movement of the slave women, saying that 'they practised the "wriggle" from such an early age that few are without it in their ordinary walking'.

A dance on the island of St Dominica, 18th-century engraving

African drums

At weekends, slaves would hold a dance that lasted right through Saturday night. Often they would trudge off to work on Monday morning, having exhausted themselves. At Christmas, slaves would have three days' holiday, during which there would be festivities known as the 'Jonkunno' (John Canoe). There was singing and dancing as a party of girls accompanied two masked men around the estates. There were similar celebrations at New Year, harvest and on a number of saints' days. Special dances were also used for courtship and marriage ceremonies.

The Europeans generally encouraged and even enjoyed slave music-making and festivities; they regarded black people as having a natural musical talent. Despite their harsh treatment of slaves, the planters realised that they needed a break and to let off steam. However, they grew to be suspicious of African drumming, believing that it was being used to communicate with slaves on other plantations and might be used to as a signal to start a revolt.

## Religion

The slaves brought with them their African religions. The Europeans felt somewhat threatened by practices they saw as a dangerous mixture of belief in spirits and magic. In particular they feared the Obeah – people who were believed to have special powers and were able to work healings and curses.

**PHILLIS WHEATLEY** was born around 1753 in Senegal on the west coast of Africa. In 1761, she was captured and deported by slave traders. She was taken to America and ended up in Boston, New England, where a tailor called John Wheatley bought her as a servant for his wife. When Phillis arrived in America she could not speak or write English, but within 16 months she had not only learned the language but was also reading English literature, the Bible, Greek and Latin classics, history and geography. At the age of thirteen she wrote her first poem. In 1773 a collection of her work entitled *Poems on Various Subjects, Religious and Moral* was published in London by Archibald Bell – the first published volume of poetry by an African-American.

> *On being brought from Africa to America*
> *'Twas mercy brought me from my* Pagan *land,*
> *Taught my benighted soul to understand*
> *That there's a God, that there's a* Saviour *too:*
> *Once I redemption neither sought nor knew,*
> *Some view our sable race with scornful eye,*
> *"Their colour is a diabolic die."*
> *Remember,* Christians, Negroes, *black as* Cain,
> *May be refin'd, and join th' angelic train.*

Phillis Wheatley, from *Poems on Various Subjects, Religious and Moral,* 1773

Despite their dislike of African religion, the planters did not try to convert the slaves to Christianity. Indeed, there was debate in the Anglican church about whether it was right to convert them at all. In fact, the Anglican church had very little effect on the slave communities. This was hardly surprising: this version of Christianity required potential converts to undergo lengthy instruction and was less concerned with a personal faith in God than with a set of rules and observances that slaves were ill-placed to follow. Not least of the obstacles was the requirement to rest completely from work on the Sabbath – a day that slaves needed for tending their own plots of land and for other tasks that simply could not be carried out during the week when they laboured for their masters. Added to this, the Anglican priests on the islands were mostly men of despicable character who were colluding with the planters.

The first major wave of slave conversions was among the colonies in North America. Nonconformist churches, with their simple message of personal salvation through faith in God succeeded where the more unwieldy doctrines of the Anglican church had failed. Many slaves flocked to hear the Baptist, Methodist and Presbyterian preachers, and were converted. The churches that grew from this movement accommodated both blacks and whites and were characterised by exuberant singing, fervent expressions of faith and the involvement of the whole congregation.

It was much later before Christianity had any impact on the slaves in the Caribbean. The first nonconformist missionaries to the islands were the Moravians. They came to Jamaica in 1754, but failed to make any significant progress. Their presentation of the gospel tended to emphasise condemnation rather than forgiveness, and offered little in the way of comfort to the suffering slaves.

The first missionary campaign to have much effect was a group of black Baptists who came to Kingston, Jamaica in the 1780s. They were led by George Leile, a black preacher and former slave from North America. They struggled against language barriers, against the deep-rooted beliefs of the African religions and against the hostility of the planters. But they became very successful and by the nineteenth century a large proportion of the slave communities were Christian.

Leile and his fellow missionaries in Jamaica were supported by missionary workers from Britain. In eighteenth-century Britain, nonconformist churches and chapels had emerged and grown rapidly. When literature from the anti-slavery movement began to deluge the country in the 1780s, it stimulated keen interest in the Caribbean slaves, especially among working class nonconformists. Converting slaves came to be seen as important work and so the new churches began to support the effort, sending both missionaries and money.

When slaves converted to Christianity, their expression of faith was characteristically African – very noisy and highly expressive. To the uneasy Europeans, it seemed uncontrolled and uncivilised. Furthermore, the churches' proclamation of the equality of all believers was highly uncomfortable for the slave owners.

## Language

The slaves who arrived on the plantations came from many different countries and regions in Africa, so there were many different native African languages among them. All had rapidly to acquire some basics of their masters' European language – misunderstanding on either side could easily lead to punishment. Across the colonies, each place developed a lingua franca – a distinctive blend of African and European languages, through which European and Africans communicated with each other. These local dialects eventually became the Creole languages of the Caribbean.

**Word origins**

**Pidgin** is the word used to describe a language that is developed in order for two groups of people to understand each other. Each group has a different native language and speaks pidgin as an additional language. The first slaves and their European masters communicated using pidgins. As children born to the slaves grew up with the pidgin as their native language, then that language became a Creole.

### Some Jamaican Creole words

A gwine: I'm going to
Annada: another
Attaclapse: a very big event, e.g. 'Lord have mercy, di police come, whatta attaclapse!'
A go: Going to do, e.g. 'Me a go tell him.'
A door: outdoors
Ackee: N. African food tree introduced about 1778. From twi ankye or kru akee.
Aks: ask
Baxide: bottom
Bigga headz: important people
Brawta: the little extra that you might get, e.g. extra sweets
Buzz: the police
Bad: good, great
Biscuit: a particularly attractive woman
Blackheart man: a rascal, a hooligan
Blouse and skirt: common exclamation of surprise
Boasie: proud, conceited, ostentatious
Boasin tone: swollen penis or testicles
Bobo: fool.
Boderation: bother
Bong belly pickney: a greedy child who eats too much
Boonoonoonous: wonderful

⊙ Points for reflection

1. Why did African culture remain so strong, even in the subsequent generations that had never lived in Africa? What was its significance in the slave society?

2. Why were slaves prepared to exhaust themselves in weekend festivities – rather than rest – when they had to face a week of hard physical labour on Monday morning?

3. What reasons would the Anglican church have had for not wanting to convert slaves to Christianity?

●→ **Find out more**

What were the obstacles to family life and how did the slaves adapt to the situations? How did the slave family change over time? What effects might their experience of family and social life have on subsequent generations? Could the effects still be evident in their descendants in the present day?

# 8

# A society under strain

In the early days of the European colonies, the workforce was a mixture of white, black and native American-Indian slaves. People of various races worked and lived together. But as the sugar plantations were established, so too was the almost exclusive use of black Africans as slave labour. Now, there was a subtly different mentality: the slave status had become identified with skin colour, and certain types of work were seen as fit only for black people. Even the shade of a slave's skin could determine how they were treated. The darker a person's skin pigmentation, the worse they were likely to be treated by the plantation owner.

## Mulattoes

As time went by, black slave mothers bore children fathered by white slave masters. The result was a slave population with a wide range of skin colours – and a corresponding system of social status. Slaves were classed according to the relative proportions of black and white blood in their parentage:

- Mulatto: the child of a black and a white.
- Sambo: the child of a mulatto and a black.
- Quadroon: the child of a mulatto and a white.
- Mustee: the child of a quadroon and a white.
- Mustifino the child of a mustee and a white.
- Quintroon: the child of a mustifino and a white.
- Octoroon: the child of a quintroon and a white (a child with such parentage was entitled to their freedom).

But the gradation in colour became the basis of a social stratification that eventually led to resentment and an obsession with race in the Caribbean colonies, even after slavery had ceased.

**Word origins**

**Mulattto** means 'mule' and was a derogatory term for people of mixed-race parentage.

Mulattoes were usually raised as slaves because their white fathers refused to recognise them. Some of these fathers, however, showed a degree of commitment to their children, and a number of mulattoes began to do well for themselves out of the financial support they received. White society, however, could only see this as a threat. Even mulatto women, as they became financially independent, were seen as a problem because white women resented the fact that white men enjoyed and sought their company.

**Population in Jamaica**

|      | Black   | White  | 'Coloured' |
|------|---------|--------|------------|
| 1768 | 167,000 | 17,000 |            |
| 1809 | 300,000 | 30,000 |            |
| 1834 | 293,128 | 15,766 | 68,529     |

Eventually white people sought to restrict the activities of mulattoes by legislation. In the eighteenth century on the island of Jamaica, a series of laws were passed that affected almost every aspect of life. Mulatto men and women were prohibited from sitting at the same table as white people and from sitting in the same section at the theatre or at church. They were no longer allowed to be buried in the same cemetery as white people, even if their white father was buried there. They were barred from the legal profession and from owning more than a certain amount of property or a certain number of slaves. They were even forbidden to wear 'white people's' clothes and jewellery, and to carry arms. They were not free to travel wherever they liked and had to obey a curfew. Moreover the legislation struck at the source of their new-found independence by limiting the amount of inheritance a mulatto could receive. Thus, racial discrimination and injustice became established in the law of the island.

## Maroon communities

As well as the plantation owners and slaves, there was another community of people living on the island of Jamaica: the Maroons. These communities of escaped slaves had started with Spanish-owned slaves who had been freed when the Spanish colonists fled from British invaders in 1660. These former slaves made their home in an area of rugged limestone mountains on the west side of the island, some distance from the sugar plantations. Over time, their numbers grew as they were joined by slaves who had run away from British owners.

There were Maroon communities on other Caribbean islands too, but the largest and most established communities were on Jamaica where the wild and mountainous terrain provided a safe retreat.

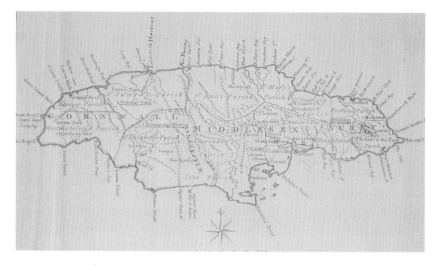

Map of Jamaica showing Maroon settlements, 1805

**Word origins**

**Maroon** from the Spanish *cimarrón*, meaning 'fugitive' and 'wild one'. The word is used in many countries, including Suriname, French Guiana, Colombia and along the United States/Mexico border.

Life on the island for the Maroons was harsh but free. They lived in villages of small cottages covered with thatch or long grass and surrounded by a fence made out of a prickly shrub. Unlike the British colonists who lived partly on an unreliable supply of imported produce, the Maroons were self-sufficient and survived by farming, hunting and gathering. They ate wild boar, fish and land crabs; they grew plantain, Indian corn or maize, cocoas, yams and other root crops. The women did most of the cultivation, just as they would have in an African village.

One piece of evidence for the Akan origins of the Maroons is the names they used. It is a West African tradition to name a baby according to the day of the week on which it is born. Jamaican Maroon names are clearly linked to Akan names, as shown in the table below.

| | Akan | Jamaican Maroon | |
|---|---|---|---|
| | | Male | Female |
| Sunday | Kwesi | Quashie | Quasheba |
| Monday | Kwadwo | Cudjoe/Kujo | Juba |
| Tuesday | Kwabena | Bene | Cobena |
| Wednesday | Kweku | Quaco | Cooba |
| Thursday | Kwau | Quaw | Aba |
| Friday | Kofi | Cuffe | Fiba |

The names have meanings, for example:

| | |
|---|---|
| Cudjoe | 'strong-headed' |
| Juba | 'clever' |
| Cuffe | 'hot-tempered' |
| Fiba | 'gentle and mild' |

**Word origins**

Many of the Maroons came from the Akan region of West Africa. The British thought the people from this area made good slaves as they were tough and disciplined. They came from a region with terrain similar to that in Jamaica, so when they escaped they were able to adapt and survive in the mountain environment. The Maroons also assimilated groups of runaways whose origins were in other regions of Africa. Over time, a Maroon language and culture evolved that was a mixture of different African traditions, but the predominant influence was Akan.

These Maroon communities were probably something of a symbol of hope for slaves in captivity on the plantations.

## The Maroon wars

From the first days of the British occupation of Jamaica, the Maroons were engaged in relentless guerrilla warfare against the British plantation owners and eventually came to represent a serious threat. They would stage raids on the plantations, burning fields, destroying property, plundering arms and ammunition and freeing slaves who would then join their community.

By the beginning of the eighteenth century, the Maroons had settled in two main groups: the Windward Maroons living on the east side of the island and the Leeward Maroons on the west side. During the seventeenth century, the number of violent confrontations in the British colonies increased and the British colonists found it difficult to cope with the attacks. Some plantation owners gave up their land and returned to Britain because of the continual assaults from Maroons on the Leeward side of the island, who were growing in numbers. The unrest culminated in the first Maroon wars, which began in 1720 and ended in 1739.

The wars finally came to an end with a peace treaty between Cudjoe, the leader of the Leeward Maroons, and Colonel Guthrie, the representative of the British Government. The government offered the assurance that the Maroons would be regarded as free people and be given 1,500 acres of land on the west side of the island. In return, the Maroons agreed to cease hostilities, to fight on the side of the British in the event of foreign invasion and to assist in the capture and return of runaways.

Maroons sign treaty with British military, late 18th century

Not everyone was happy about the agreement. One objector was Nanny, the legendary Maroon leader of the Windward Maroons. Tradition has it that she had piercing eyes and apparent supernatural powers, which she used when planning guerrilla warfare against the British between 1728 and 1734. These alleged powers included an ability to 'attract and catch bullets with her buttocks and render them harmless'.

The truce worked reasonably well until 1795 when the new Governor of Jamaica, the Earl of Balcarres, began to persecute people in the Maroon town of Trelawny. When he had two residents flogged, a group of Maroons revolted and the result was the Second Maroon War. At the beginning, the Maroon fighters were at an advantage because they were more familiar with the wild and mountainous territory. The British, however, brought in reinforcements including several thousand militia and 100 bloodhounds, and eventually prevailed. With defeat looming, the Maroons consented to a meeting with a Major General Walpole, a British leader whom they trusted. He agreed that they should be given new lands and would not be executed or transported. With the agreement in view, they gave themselves up at

Runaway slave being attacked by dogs, 19th century

Montego Bay, only to find that the promises made meant nothing to Governor Balcarres or the Assembly. One year after the start of the war, the government deported 568 Maroons from Trelawny to Nova Scotia, and three years later from thence to Sierra Leone. None of them ever returned to Jamaica.

The defeat and subsequent deportation of the Trelawny Maroons acted as a deterrent to would-be rebel fighters. The Maroons became more cooperative, helping the government to control slave runaways and rebellions.

The established Maroon communities endured and a few survive in the present day, although some have retained their Akan culture more strongly than others.

---

### ⊙ Points for reflection

1. Why would such a detailed classification for people of different parentage exist? What does it reveal about these Caribbean island societies?

2. Why were the financially independent Mulattoes seen as a threat by the colonialists?

3. Why were the Maroons so disliked by the plantation owners?

---

### ●→ Find out more

---

Where are the present-day Maroon communities? How do they compare with Maroon communities in the time of slavery?

---

# 9

# Ending the trade

In the middle of the eighteenth century, the slave-powered plantations in the West Indies were providing munificent supplies of tropical produce that satisfied British appetites and boosted the British economy. Sugar, in particular, was being consumed in ever-increasing quantities. The slave trade itself, on which the plantations relied for fresh supplies of labour, was also a source of financial gain. British interests were being generously served by the whole system. Yet, by the end of the century, the movement to abolish the trade had not only been started, but was well on the way to achieving its goal. How did this happen in such a relatively short time? The reasons are fiercely debated by historians: some point to the dedication of the band of Christian campaigners; others believe the true causes were political and economic. It seems likely that a number of events and circumstances were contributory factors.

## A changing climate

In the eighteenth century the world was changing. The European movement known as 'The Enlightenment' had set the stage for broader ideological debates about human rights, equality, free trade – all of which had implications for slavery. In Britain, the Industrial Revolution meant that the issue of labour was seen in a new light. Set against British manufacturers talking about free labour and free trade, slavery looked increasingly like an embarrassing anomaly.

The nonconformist movement in the Church brought about a further change in social mood. The early part of the century saw the founding of Baptist and Methodist chapels in towns and cities across the country. With their emphasis on personal morality and on the active involvement of the whole congregation, these new churches were empowering their members and spurring them into social and political action.

The founder of the Methodist movement, John Wesley, was a vociferous critic of the slave trade. Having come into contact with slaves when he visited North America in 1736, he had become opposed to slavery long before the issue became a matter of public concern. His subsequent research and conversations with people involved in the slave trade served to strengthen his views, and in 1774 he published a booklet, *Thoughts Upon Slavery*. Following this publication, John Wesley continued to make his views known and was a great influence on political leaders such as William Wilberforce.

> *Are you a man? Then you should have an human heart. But have you indeed? What is your heart made of? Is there no such principle as compassion there? Do you never feel another's pain? Have you no sympathy, no sense of human woe, no pity for the miserable? When you saw the flowing eyes, the heaving breasts, or the bleeding sides and tortured limbs of your fellow-creatures, was you a stone, or a brute? Did you look upon them with the eyes of a tiger? When you squeezed the agonizing creatures down in the ship, or when you threw their poor mangled remains into the sea, had you no relenting? Did not one tear drop from your eye, one sigh escape from your breast? Do you feel no relenting now? If you do not, you must go on, till the measure of your iniquities is full. Then will the great God deal with you as you have dealt with them, and require all their blood at your hands ...*
>
> *O, whatever it costs, put a stop to its cry before it be too late: Instantly, at any price, were it the half of your goods, deliver thyself from blood-guiltiness! Thy hands, thy bed, thy furniture, thy house, thy lands, are at present stained with blood. Surely it is enough; accumulate no more guilt; spill no more the blood of the innocent! Do not hire another to shed blood; do not pay him for doing it! Whether you are a Christian or no, show yourself a man! Be not more savage than a lion or a bear!*
>
> Extract from *Thoughts Upon Slavery*, John Wesley, 1774

Against the backdrop of changing ideology and awakened social conscience, the plight of African slaves was being thrust increasingly under the noses of the British people. In the mid-eighteenth century, there were several court cases over slave ship insurance claims. Cases such as that of the infamous slave ship, the *Zong*, brought the grim and shocking details of the slave trade to the attention of the press and the public.

Granville Sharp

In addition, there was also the increasing problem of the legal position of black slaves who landed up in Britain. The question was: could slave owners force their slaves into returning to the colonies? A test case brought in 1771 by the humanitarian Granville Sharp resulted in the judgement that the slave in question, James Somerset, was free to remain in Britain and was not bound by his master's wish for him to return. The judge had not proclaimed freedom for all British slaves, but this case and others served to highlight the uncomfortable situation in Britain with regard to slavery.

## The Society for the Abolition of the Slave Trade

The first group to make a concerted attack on the institution of slavery was the Society of Friends, a nonconformist Christian movement started in 1643 by George Fox. The Society of Friends, who became known as the Quakers, believed strongly in the equality of all people and became very active in social and political reform. They put forward their first objections to slavery in the late 1600s, produced the first anti-slavery literature in the 1760s and presented their first anti-slavery petition to parliament in 1763.

In 1787 they joined forces with the humanitarian campaigner Granville Sharp and a young friend of his called Thomas Clarkson to launch the Society for the Abolition of the Slave Trade. Initially their call was simply for the abolition of the Atlantic slave trade – not for an end to slavery itself. The arguments were based on both religious and humanitarian grounds. The abolitionists supported their argument with the suggestion that the economic gap left by slave trade could be filled, in part, by free trade with Africa, which was a rich source of natural commodities.

Thomas Clarkson

The campaign was well organised and extremely vigorous. Lectures and meetings were held across the country, signatures were gathered onto petitions and MPs were lobbied. The society showered the country with books and pamphlets that described the atrocities of the slave trade and argued for its abolition. The literature drew on factual information gained first-hand from people who had been involved with the trade. It also used poems and ballads, such as *The Negro's Complaint* by William Cowper. The society's motto – Am I not a friend and a brother? – pointed unmistakeably to the underlying issue: the denial of the slaves' humanity.

The driving force behind the movement was, without any doubt, Thomas Clarkson. Between 1787 and 1794, he travelled 35,000 miles on horseback, meticulously compiling evidence to support the crusade. He visited ports, examined and recorded details of the slave vessels in the docks, and interviewed 20,000 sailors to get first-hand accounts of life on board and of treatment of slaves. He also collected artefacts such as handcuffs, shackles, thumbscrews, instruments for force-feeding and branding irons. As the campaign's call for abolition was linked to proposals for free trade, he also gathered information that helped to demonstrate the possibilities for free trade with Africa. He published his findings via books and pamphlets, persuaded newspaper editors to carry articles, and also reported to parliament.

As Clarkson travelled, he rallied support for the cause by speaking to large crowds and talking to influential people. It has been suggested that such was

A seal depicting the emblem of the Society for the Abolition of the Slave Trade, designed by Josiah Wedgwood. The motto reads, 'Am I not a friend and a brother?'

the effectiveness of his tour, by 1792 there were 400,000 British people boycotting slave-produced sugar. Clarkson continued his efforts unstintingly until 1794, when illness brought on by overwork forced him to stop.

The anti-slavery movement quickly took hold across the whole country, thanks to the network of Quaker groups and the fervent activities of many women.

## Voices of the oppressed and the oppressors

Added to the chorus of anti-slavery campaigners were the voices of slaves who had managed to gain their freedom and were now able to tell of their experiences. The most well known are probably those of Olaudah Equiano and Ottabah Cugoano.

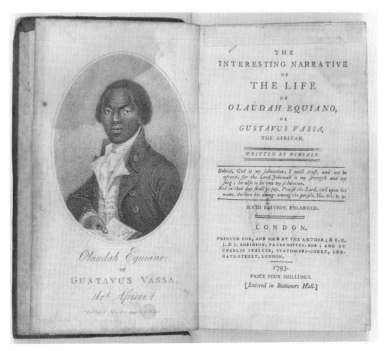

The title page of Olaudah Equiano's autobiography

**OLAUDAH EQUIANO** Kidnapped from an African village at the age of 11, Olaudah Equiano was taken to Barbados and then to Virginia. He was eventually sold to a British naval officer and thus travelled to many parts of the world, gaining experience of naval warfare as well a good education. He was sold again to an owner on the Caribbean island of Montserrat and it was here that he witnessed the most terrible abuse of slaves. Through his work as a slave, he managed to save enough money to buy his freedom, and after further travelling eventually returned to London.

Back in Britain, Equiano became involved with the abolitionist movement and in 1789 he published his autobiography, *The Interesting Narrative of the Life of Olaudah Equiano*. The book gave a detailed account of slave experience and set out the arguments against slavery. As a well-written narrative it also stood as a repudiation of the idea, held by some British people, that black Africans were somehow less human and not as intellectually developed as white people.

*Population, the bowels and surface of Africa, abound in valuable and useful returns; the hidden treasures of centuries will be brought to light and into circulation. Industry, enterprise, and mining, will have their full scope, proportionably as they civilise. In a word, it lays open an endless field of commerce to the British manufacturers and merchant adventurers. The manufacturing interest and the general interests are synonymous. The abolition of slavery would be in reality an universal good.*

*Tortures, murder, and every other imaginable barbarity and iniquity are practised upon the poor slaves with impunity. I hope the slave-trade will be abolished. I pray it may be an event at hand. The great body of manufacturers, uniting in the cause, will considerably facilitate and expedite it; and, as I have already stated, it is most substantially their interest and advantage, and as such the nation's at large (except those persons concerned in the manufacturing neck-yokes, collars, chains, hand-cuffs, leg-bolts, drags, thumb screws, iron-muzzles, and coffins; cats, scourges, and other instruments of torture used in the slave-trade).*

Extract from *The Interesting Narrative of the Life of Olaudah Equiano*, 1789

There was no shortage of people who had been involved in the slave trade coming forward to testify to the gruesome realities of life on board the slave ships. John Newton was a sea captain who became an Anglican priest. He was later to write many hymns, including *Amazing Grace*.

> During the time I was engaged in the slave trade, I never had the least scruple to its lawfulness. I was upon the whole satisfied with it as the appointment providence had marked out for me. It was indeed counted a genteel employment, usually very profitable, though to me it did not prove so, the Lord seeing that a large increase of wealth would not be good for me. However, I considered myself as a sort of jailer and I was sometimes shocked with an employment that was perpetually connected with chains, bolts, and shackles. In this view I had often prayed that the Lord, in His own time would place me in a more humane calling, and where I might have more frequent fellowship with His people and ordinances.
>
> John Newton

> I have been informed that some commanders have cut off the legs or arms of the most wilful slaves, to terrify the rest, for they believe that, if they lose a member, they cannot return home again: I was advised by some of my officers to do the same, but I could not be persuaded to entertain the least thought of it, much less to put in practice such barbarity and cruelty to poor creatures who, excepting their want of Christianity and true religion (their misfortune more than fault), are as much the works of God's hands, and no doubt as dear to him as ourselves.
>
> Thomas Phillips (slave-ship captain), *A Journal of a Voyage*, 1746

## Political change

In 1787, Thomas Clarkson met the politician William Wilberforce and asked him to lead the parliamentary campaign for the abolition of slavery. Wilberforce had a brilliant mind as well as being eloquent and charming. As a convert to evangelical Christianity, he was known to approach politics from a standpoint of Christian morality. Wilberforce agreed to the proposition, knowing that he would have the support of the prime minister, William Pitt the Younger, who was also opposed to slavery.

Using information supplied by Thomas Clarkson, Wilberforce brought the evidence before parliament. In 1789, he made a momentous speech to the House of Commons, presenting the Abolition Bill.

William Wilberforce

*I mean not to accuse anyone, but to take the shame upon myself, in common, indeed, with the whole parliament of Great Britain, for having suffered this horrid trade to be carried on under their authority. We are all guilty, we ought all to plead guilty, and not to exculpate ourselves by throwing the blame on others; and I therefore deprecate every kind of reflection against the various descriptions of people who are more immediately involved in this wretched business ...*

*What will the House think when, by the concurring testimony of other witnesses, the true history is laid open? The slaves who are sometimes described as rejoicing at their captivity, are so wrung with misery at leaving their country, that it is the constant practice to set sail at night, lest they should be sensible of their departure. The pulse which Mr. Norris talks of are horse beans; and the scantiness, both of water and provision, was suggested by the very legislature of Jamaica in the report of their committee, to be a subject that called for the interference of parliament. Mr. Norris talks of frankincense and lime juice; when the surgeons tell you the slaves are stowed so close, that there is not room to tread among them: and when you have it in evidence from Sir George Yonge, that even in a ship which wanted 200 of her complement, the stench was intolerable. The song and the dance, says Mr. Norris, are promoted. It had been more fair, perhaps, if he had explained that word promoted. The truth is, that for the sake of exercise, these miserable wretches, loaded with chains, oppressed with disease and wretchedness, are forced to dance by the terror of the lash, and sometimes by the actual use of it.*

William Wilberforce, Speech to the House of Commons,
Tuesday 12 May 1789

## Setback

Following Wilberforce's speech, many people thought that the end was in sight, but there followed a series of parliamentary delays as evidence from the opposition was heard. The motion was narrowly outvoted on several occasions. Then, in 1791, news of the slave revolts in St Domingue (Haiti) reached Britain and many people became more cautious about abolition. The situation in the West Indies was clearly volatile and they thought it dangerous to tamper with the system. They saw the violence as evidence of what happened when slaves were not kept under strict control and their true nature was allowed free rein. The slave trade, meanwhile, was as brisk as ever: in 1793 a record 23,000 new slaves arrived in Jamaica alone.

At the end of the eighteenth century, the situation across much of Europe was looking very unstable. The French Revolution in 1789 and the Jacobite Rebellions had made people uneasy and the abolitionists found themselves contending with increasing doubt and opposition. For a few years the movement to abolish slavery appeared to have foundered. Then, in 1803, Thomas Clarkson, who had retired from his abolitionist activities in 1794 owing to ill health, rejoined the committee. The campaign was relaunched and William Wilberforce brought the bill back to parliament. On 23 February 1807, the bill to abolish the slave trade was passed with an overwhelming majority. It was now illegal for any British ship to trade in slaves.

> **OTTOBAH CUGOANO** Born around 1757 in Ghana, Ottobah Cugoano was deported as a slave when he was about thirteen years old. After working on plantations in the Caribbean, he was taken to England where he was set free. As a free man he worked as a servant to the artist Richard Cosway and learned to read and write. He wrote *Thoughts and Sentiments on the Evil and Wicked Traffic of the Commerce of the Human Species*, the first major English anti-slavery text by an African, which was published in 1787.

**IGNATIUS SANCHO** Born aboard a slave ship in 1729, Ignatius Sancho was taken to England aged two. He became a servant to the Duke of Montagu who was taken with the child's intelligence and disposition and encouraged his love of reading. Eventually Sancho received an inheritance from the Montagu family that enabled him to set up his own grocery shop on Charles Street, Westminster.

A self-educated man, Sancho wrote poetry, composed music and became a respected figure in the literary, musical and artistic circles of eighteenth-century London. He sought to bring the inhumanity of slavery to the attention of the British people. In 1782, two years after his death, his letters were published in a book and quickly became a bestseller. Ignatius Sancho was the first African writer to have his work published in England. His intellect and eloquence appealed to the educated classes and clearly refuted the commonly held view that black people were innately less intelligent.

---

### ⊙ Points for reflection

1. What does John Wesley's writing reveal about the man and his beliefs? What are his main arguments against slavery? How would people at the time be likely to react to his suggestions?

2. What are Olaudah Equiano's arguments for the abolition of the slave trade? What does the extract reveal about him?

3. What does William Wilberforce's speech suggest about what the British public had been told about slaves? Where would the information have come from? Is it likely that it was believed? What does the speech reveal about Wilberforce and his attitude?

---

### ●→ Find out more

What social, political and economic conditions set the stage for the abolition of slavery? What, if any, were the influential changes in thinking produced by the Enlightenment?

---

# 10

# The fight for freedom

An Act of Parliament in 1807 abolished the slave trade, but not slavery itself. About 600,000 Africans and their descendants were still working as slaves in the Caribbean. The abolitionists hoped that with no further supplies of Africans, plantation owners would treat their slaves better and that free labour would develop. After a few years, however, it became apparent that as far as the slaves were concerned, nothing had really changed. Reports from nonconformist missionaries confirmed that the planters were continuing to abuse their slaves, just as before.

In 1823 the Anti-Slavery Society was formed and the campaigning began again. Thomas Clarkson and William Wilberforce were involved in the early stages, but both were now older and in poor health. When Wilberforce retired in 1825, the MP Sir Thomas Fowell Buxton took over the parliamentary campaign.

At first the aim was to try and improve conditions for the slaves, but this was quickly superseded by the call for emancipation.

## Unrest in the Caribbean

While the abolition campaign was gathering pace in Britain, there was a social change taking place in the West Indian colonies that would play a significant part in the ending of slavery. Following the arrival of nonconformist missionaries in the 1780s, slaves were being converted to Christianity in their thousands. It is estimated that between 1800 and 1825, there were approximately a quarter of a million slave converts. In 1815, legislation was passed that gave slaves the right to receive religious instruction.

The surge in black Christianity had several consequences. In the chapels and

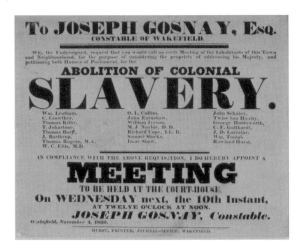

Handbill advertising anti-slavery meeting

churches, slaves found not only an attractive alternative society, but also the opportunity for education and instruction. Through Sunday schools and Bible classes, many slaves learned to read and write. The Biblical messages of salvation, freedom and the equality of believers gave them hope and determination. As a result of the church's teaching, slaves no longer saw themselves as inferior to their masters. From these congregations emerged empowered black leaders – charismatic figures who were able to rally and inspire their communities.

The planters observed this social revolution with growing unease. They persecuted the white missionaries and made life difficult for the Christian slaves. However, this did nothing for their cause. Back in Britain, public opinion had shifted: now that slaves were largely Christian, they were attracting increasing public sympathy. The planters were now seen as the villains.

The unrest gave rise to various slave revolts. The biggest and most violent of these was the so-called 'Baptist War' (also known as the 'Christmas Rebellion') that took place on Jamaica in 1831. It was led by Sam Sharpe, a black slave in a position of leadership in the Baptist church, known for his powerful and persuasive preaching. Sharpe believed that the planters were conspiring to burn official documents that granted slaves' freedom. He persuaded the slaves to stage a strike, against the wishes of the pastor of his own church, the Reverend Knibb.

Slaves setting fire to a plantation

Reverend Knibb appealed to the striking slaves in 1831 with this speech:

> *I am pained – pained to the soul, at being told that many of you have agreed not to go to work any more for your owners, and I fear this is too true. I learn that some wicked persons have persuaded you that the King of England has made you free. Hear me! I love your souls and I would not tell you a lie for the whole world; I assure you that it is false, false as hell can make it. I entreat you not to believe it, but go to your work as formerly. If you have any love to Jesus Christ, to religion, to your ministers, or to those kind friends in England who have helped you to build this chapel, and who are sending a minister for you, do not be led away. God commands you to be obedient.*

Sam Sharpe's reply:

> *We have worked enough already and will no more; the life we live is too bad, it is the life of a dog, we won't be slaves no more, we won't lift hoe no more, we won't take flogging any more.*

However, Sharpe's plans for a peaceful strike were overturned by slaves who saw the opportunity for revolt. Starting on the Kensington estate in the parish of St James, they set fire to plantations and the peaceful protest soon escalated into a violent conflict that spread across western Jamaica. The militia reacted quickly and within a few days the rebellion had been quashed. Fourteen white people died, but over 1,000 slaves were either killed in the conflict or hanged afterwards. Bodies were piled up in Montego Bay Square before being buried in mass graves. Sam Sharpe was hanged on 6 February 1832.

## Through apprenticeship to freedom

By the time of the Baptist War, the abolitionist campaign in Britain had won over the majority of public opinion. Many British people were outraged by the death of Sam Sharpe and the slave massacre, and the conflict in Jamaica provided further evidence that the system was crumbling. A week after Sam Sharpe had been hanged, the British parliament appointed a committee to look into ways of ending slavery.

In 1832, there was a parliamentary reform act and a new Whig government under Lord Grey, who was in favour of black freedom. Many MPs in both Houses were willing to support an abolition bill, and this paved the way for the Emancipation Act. The bill was read in the House of Commons in July 1833 – three days before the death of William Wilberforce, the man who had been instrumental in bringing in anti-slavery legislation. The act was finally passed in 1834.

There had been much debate about how emancipation should be brought in: the concern was that the planters should not be deprived of labour, literally overnight. When it was finally passed, the act decreed that all children under the age of six would be free with immediate effect; all other slaves would become 'apprentices'. This meant that they would have to work another six years for their owners before gaining full freedom. They would be given lodging, clothes, food and medical attention in return for forty hours' labour a week. Slaves were allowed to hire themselves out in their free time and if they saved enough money would be allowed to buy their freedom. The planters were to be paid £20 million in compensation. No compensation was paid to slaves, abolitionists pointed out.

There were fears that once freedom was granted, slaves would wreak revenge on their owners. In the event, there were no recriminations. On the night of 31 July 1834, slaves flocked into the churches and chapels to attend all-night vigils. When midnight came, exuberant celebrations broke out.

The apprentice scheme was intended to provide a period of transition, but it was flagrantly abused by the plantation owners. They exploited the

Procession celebrating the abolition of slavery in Jamaica

slaves, many of whom resisted apprenticeship and refused to work for no wages. The scheme was therefore brought to an early end, and full freedom was granted on 31 July 1838. Once more, slaves crowded into the churches overnight to hold services and await the day of freedom. In Spanish Town, the capital of Jamaica, the governor read the proclamation of the abolition of slavery and the 311,000 black and coloured people on the island celebrated with parades, music, speeches, feasting and fireworks.

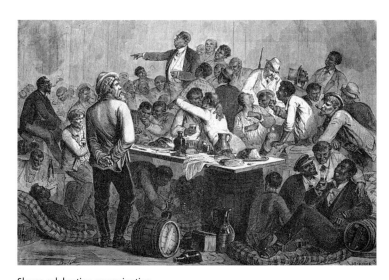

Slaves celebrating emancipation

⊙    Points for reflection

1. Why did people in Britain see slaves in such a different light once they had become Christian?

2. What does Reverend Knibb's speech indicate about his attitude towards slavery?

3. The 'Baptist War' appeared to galvanise the British government into action over slavery. What are the likely reasons for this?

4. What were the reasons for the failure of the apprenticeship scheme? What might the government of the day have done to provide a more successful means of transition?

●→ **Find out more**

What was attractive about Christianity for enslaved people? How did conversion to Christianity affect the slave communities? What positive effects did it have? What problems resulted, if any?

# Loosing the shackles

# 11

Slavery in British colonies finally came to an end in 1838, but it was still practised by other nations. Having gathered momentum in the years leading up to emancipation in the British colonies, the British Anti-Slavery Society continued to campaign against slave trading and systems of slavery in other parts of the world.

## Britain takes up the cause

Between 1820 and 1870, the British Royal Navy seized over 1,500 ships, freeing 150,000 slaves who had been destined for the Caribbean and the Americas. Britain's interests were not entirely unselfish, however: they hoped that ending the transatlantic slave trade would open the way for free trade with Africa.

In fact, Britain had not been the first country to abolish its slave trade. Denmark had ended its more modest trade in 1803. The Dutch trade, which had largely stopped during war with France at the end of the eighteenth century, was officially ended in 1814. The French slave trade stopped after about 1831, but slavery in French colonies continued until 1848.

The last nation to put an end to slavery was the country that had led Europe into the slave trade over three centuries earlier. Portugal formally abolished slavery in 1876, although in many of the Portuguese colonies slaves were liberated only very gradually through systems similar to the British apprenticeship.

In the southern states of North America, slavery was entrenched. After the introduction of cotton in the early years of the nineteenth century, cotton production quickly took off – powered by black slaves.

Britain started to crusade against the slaving systems of other countries, apparently forgetting their own extremely recent involvement. They self-righteously vaunted the abolition of British slavery, conveniently leaving aside the fact that it was their own actions that had brought about the terrible situation in the first place. Other countries, notably France, saw Britain's stance as hypocritical.

There is also evidence that while the British campaigned for the abolition of slave trading in other countries, it was still being supported in some quarters in Britain. British banks appear to have given credit to slave traders as well as to slave-driven mines and plantations in the Americas, and British underwriters were still insuring slave vessels – some of which were being built in Britain. One company in Birmingham continued to produce the iron collars and shackles used on slaves. Slavery on British territory had officially been abolished, but the roots of the system extended deep into the fabric of the nation and would take time to eradicate.

## The new order in the colonies

Following the disappearance of slave labour, prosperity in British Caribbean colonies rapidly declined. The shift from slave labour to a waged workforce caused economic and social chaos. Planters no longer had a guaranteed source of labour and slaves were not keen to work for the meagre wages they offered.

For the former slaves, the reality of free life was harsh and insecure. Slave owners had provided the basics of life – housing, food and clothing – albeit very frugally. As free workers they now had to eke out a living from the pittance paid by the plantation owners. Some slaves became peasant smallholders, scraping a living by subsistence farming on small plots that they bought, rented or obtained through squatting. Some were helped with their purchase by money sent from charities in England.

Others were anxious to move away from the plantations that had enslaved them for so long, and migrated to find employment. Former slaves and their descendants went to work on the sugar and tobacco plantations in Cuba, on the banana plantations in Central America and on the building of the railway and canal in Panama.

Request for donations by a Christian charity

## A society still divided

There had been much energy devoted to the campaign for abolition of slavery, but little consideration given to the rehabilitation of slaves once freedom had been won. Abolitionists had imagined that former slaves would be able to flourish in a thriving system of free labour and that they would work hard in return for wages. They had not taken into account the fact that the attitudes and behaviours that resulted from the slaving system had become deeply entrenched: neither planters nor slaves knew anything else.

The planters' attitude towards black people therefore remained much as it had been when they were slaves. The former slaves, for their part, had been accustomed only to enforced working under the threat of violent punishment; they had no experience of the self-discipline required of free workers. Furthermore, uncertain employment and low wages provided little incentive to cultivate a work ethic. Consequently white people came to regard black workers as 'lazy'. Some even saw the reluctance of black workers as proof that African people were naturally indolent and required the discipline of slavery. British people, including the abolitionists, became disillusioned and disappointed when the freedom they had fought for did not turn out the way they had hoped.

> A slaveholder does not acknowledge by any other power over his slave than his own. God's commandments, convictions and conscience, he will and does, set a defiance – he laughs at them. Even after slavery had been abolished, I had once to plead the cause of a former slave against his master, who had ordered him to do what was awfully sinful. 'This man,' I said, 'knows it and feels it to be wrong: how then can you expect him to do it?' 'What,' he answered, 'Did not I tell him? What business has he to think, or to judge, or to set up his conscience after I have commanded him!' Yes, the slaveholder demands obedience of body and soul …
>
> The Reverend Buchner

Black people may now have been technically 'free', but they found themselves in a society where discrimination and injustice were still part of the fabric of the system and where racism was institutionalised. The plantation owners still held all the power. They sought to control black workers by manipulating the tax laws to their advantage, and exploited them by paying wages of less than a shilling a day. Faced with intolerable poverty, many black people were forced to steal – and those who ended up in court inevitably faced an unfair trial.

The church did its best to unite the new society, but many of its actions were badly misguided and in the end only created further division. Many of the former slaves had been converted to Christianity within the nonconformist movement, and churches and chapels had become the focus of many slave communities. Ministers in the churches had provided education and – after emancipation – land to establish villages for the freed slaves. Nevertheless, the Christian culture they promoted was also white culture. Thus white culture came to be upheld as the way to God, and African culture seen as having no particular place in a Christian community.

Following emancipation, black communities began to develop a stronger sense of ethnic identity as cultural roots and land ownership took on a new importance. In asserting their own culture, many black people rejected some of the church's trappings such as education and Christian marriage. The black community's model of family life was different from that presented by the church as 'Christian' (although this was largely derived from white western culture rather than from anything in the Bible). In the black community, mutual commitment based on the sharing of responsibilities was the basis of a family into which children were born. White 'Christian marriage' with its subordination of women did not fit well with black society, and a church wedding – which was expensive in any case – was often not seen as particularly important. This frequently led to difficulties when church leaders labelled those they regarded as unmarried fathers as social outcasts and refused to baptise their children whom they regarded as illegitimate.

In the Baptist church some people broke away to form a separate group, known as the 'native Baptists'. Their distinctively African style of worship and apparent lack of concern for education met with strong disapproval from the rest of the nonconformist church.

## Jamaica post-slavery

When full freedom was granted on 1 August 1838, there were over 300,000 slaves working on Jamaica's sugar plantations. The island continued to be governed by the Jamaican House of Assembly, a parliament of elected representatives presided over by an appointed governor. Only white people and mulattoes could stand for election and only property owners were allowed to vote – which excluded nearly all black people. This meant that political power was largely in the hands of the plantocracy. The relationship between planters and labourers had changed but, as in the other British colonies, it was troubled. Housing and rent were particular sources of conflict.

A number of individuals, many of them nonconformist ministers, tried to ease the situation by establishing villages for the freed slaves, near to the plantations. They bought areas of land and sold housing lots to the workers. Sligoville, named after the Marquis of Sligo who was governor of Jamaica from 1834 to 1836, is believed to be the first of these villages. Many others soon sprang up. The Reverend James Phillippo, a Baptist Minister, bought 25 acres at Mount Pleasant where he provided a village with a chapel and a school. Sturge Town was named after a Joseph Sturge, a Quaker. The people at Sturge Town cultivated produce that was sold in Brown's Town markets along the coastal sugar belt to the north. The Baptist Minister John Clarke purchased land in St Ann and named it Clarksonville, after the abolitionist, Thomas Clarkson. He established five free villages in all. The Baptist minister William Knibb purchased 90 acres of land for a settlement that was named Granville, after Granville Sharpe the abolitionist. He also established other villages such as the Alps, Hoby Town, Hastings and part of Duncan, Refuge and Kettering (named after Knibb's own birthplace).

To own land was a sign of freedom and the newly established villages gave many ex-slaves the opportunity to establish themselves on their own plots. However, the plots were very small – too small to cultivate – and many workers still felt they were enjoying a poor sort of independence. As landowners, some were entitled to vote and the black peasant farmers gradually began to have some political influence on the island, albeit a limited one.

## The Morant Bay Rebellion

In the years after emancipation the economic situation in Jamaica steadily worsened. Previously, sugar from British colonies had not been subject to the heavy import duties levied on sugar from other colonies. When Britain adopted a policy of free trade in 1848, Jamaican sugar was no longer subsidised in this way and it became increasingly difficult to compete with sugar from places such as Cuba, where slave labour was still being used. As sugar was being produced from sugar beet, cultivation was no longer confined to the tropics, and this also increased competition.

By the 1860s there was increasing dissatisfaction and disillusionment in various parts of Jamaican society. The situation was made worse by the appointment of Edward John Eyre as governor in 1862. He increased taxes and made himself unpopular with everyone including the politicians. Eventually the growing unrest on the island spilled over into rebellion.

One of the leaders to emerge from the black peasant communities was Paul Bogle, a smallholder and a deacon in the Native Baptist church in the district of Stony Gut. He was an ally and supporter of George William Gordon, one of the coloured members of the Jamaican parliament. Born a slave, but freed by his father who was a Scottish planter, Gordon had become a successful businessman and landowner. He was also a Baptist minister and worked to improve the lot of the poor, setting up fairer systems for them to market their produce, and selling them land at reduced rates.

In October 1865 Paul Bogle and some of his followers went to the courthouse at Morant Bay to support two men standing trial. Bogle and his men came to the defence of a man who was being arrested for calling out during the hearing. Later, police came to Stony Gut to arrest Paul Bogle, but they were fought off by the people of the town. Bogle then led a group of around 200 black men and women to Morant Bay to challenge the white ruling class. They were confronted by the militia, who opened fire, killing seven protesters. Fighting broke out. The protesters set fire to the courthouse and took control of the town. The rebellion quickly spread to the surrounding countryside, with over 2,000 rebels joining the fight and setting fire to plantations. The rebellion was brutally suppressed by guards under the leadership of Governor Eyre. Bogle and his followers returned to Stony Gut, but when troops arrived the town and the chapel were destroyed. Bogle and Gordon were arrested and taken back to Morant Bay to stand trial. Gordon was accused of helping to plan the rebellion and when questioned about his part in the uprising, he said, 'No, friend, I never gave the people bad advice; I only told them the Lord would send them a day of deliverance.' He was hanged, along with Paul Bogle and 438 other protesters. Another 600 were flogged and thousands of black workers' homes were burnt to the ground.

In Britain, news of the brutal suppression of the riots provoked outrage and the British government called an inquiry into the causes of the rebellion. As a result, they abolished the Jamaican House of Assembly, replacing it with a crown colony government. This meant that the island was ruled by a Legislative Council consisting of members appointed by the crown. There would still be an appointed governor who was to have increased powers.

In 1866 Sir John Peter Grant was sent from India to be the governor of Jamaica and to set up the new organisation. The 22 parishes into which the island had been divided were reduced to 14. The police force was reorganised

Morant Bay rebellion

and district courts established with judges who were officers of the crown. It was hoped that this would result in a fairer system of law and justice.

New policies were introduced to try and resolve conflicts over land ownership, but the new laws meant that many black farmers who had paid for land, but did not have the necessary documentation, were evicted.

## The changing Caribbean society

Deprived of a large part of their workforce, plantation owners looked elsewhere for labour. Thousands of indentured labourers were shipped from India. These were poor people who had been offered work and the chance to buy land. Although they were free to return after five years, few of them did, and many reverted to their former occupations, which included fishing, metalworking and moneylending. Between 1845 and 1917, over a half a million Indians were taken to the British colonies under a system that bore some noticeable similarities to the recently abolished Atlantic trade. People of East Indian origin are now the largest ethnic minority group in Jamaica and other parts of the Caribbean. These immigrants introduced various plants from India, including betel, coolie plum, mango, jackfruit and tamarind, many of which became part of the Caribbean diet.

Indentured labour also came from other countries in the same period. Immigrants from China formed a relatively small proportion of the population but became quite influential owing to their success in setting up small grocery shops across Jamaica. Many people with Chinese origins can be found in present-day retail businesses on the island.

German labourers arrived mainly during the period of apprenticeship (1834–1838). They, and other European immigrants, were treated favourably because they were not black. Planters gave them the best land in the mistaken hope that they would provide a good example for the ex-slaves.

Middle East immigrants came from Lebanon, Syria and Palestine, fleeing the oppression in Turkey. Initially they went into growing bananas and then into retail.

The other significant ethnic group on the island are Jews. They first came to the island between 1494 and 1655, fleeing the Spanish Inquisition in Spain and Portugal. Remaining fearful of persecution, they called themselves Portuguese and practised their religion in secret. Gradually their true identity was recognised and accepted, and in 1831 they were given full political rights, which included the right to own property. Although a relatively small group, their contribution to the economic and commercial life of Jamaica is comparable to that of groups with much greater numbers.

After over 400 years of people arriving from all over the world, by the beginning of the twentieth century the Caribbean islands had become societies of remarkable ethnic variety.

## Africa

The effect of the European slave trade on African states was profound. Slavery had existed in Africa previously, but the trade that grew up in response to the demands of the Atlantic system was on a much larger scale. It affected not only the coastal ports and trading centres but also countries and communities deep in Africa's interior. Agricultural communities were devastated and three states collapsed completely. The trade fanned the flames of internal conflict, causing war and hostility among neighbouring states and communities as Africans literally sold each other into slavery.

The consequences of the turmoil and the loss to communities were undoubtedly enormous, but it is extremely difficult to calculate the extent of the loss in economic terms with any degree of certainty. It has been estimated that if there had been no slave trade, the population of Africa in 1850 would have been nearer to 50 million instead of 25 million. It is even more difficult to deduce the effects of the loss of so many young people from societies. Industrial production certainly suffered because of the disappearance of so many young men, and many historians believe the slave trade is one of the main reasons for the lack of industrial and economic development in some regions.

### ⊙ Points for reflection

1. Was Britain right to crusade against the slave trade of other countries? Did their past activity in the trade affect their right to intervene?

2. How might the slaves' experience of freedom have compared with the hopes and expectations before emancipation? What would be the effects of a lifetime in slavery – on individuals and on families and communities? How would the experience affect people's ability to cope with the different demands of a free life?

3. How would Caribbean society be affected by the many immigrants from different countries and cultures? What are the special features of such a cosmopolitan country and its citizens?

### ●→ Find out more

How does Jamaica's culture reflect its cosmopolitan population?

# 12

# Black presence in Britain up to 1900

For the past 2,000 years, Britain has been a multicultural society. The first people to invade Britain were the Romans, who extended their empire into Britain in 43 AD. At that time Britain was inhabited by various tribes who spoke Celtic languages. By 410 the Romans had departed, and for the next two centuries invaders arrived from northern Europe. The Jutes and Angles came from modern-day Denmark, and the Saxons from an area further west. These groups, who all spoke Germanic languages, were known collectively as Anglo-Saxons. They settled in the south and east of Britain, while the north and west were still inhabited mainly by Celtic peoples.

In 789 there was a further wave of invasions, this time from Scandinavia. From Denmark and Norway, the Vikings made violent raids on the coast of Britain. Eventually they settled in several areas of the country; Danish Vikings gravitating to the east and Norwegians to Scotland, Ireland and north-west England. In 1066 Britain was conquered by the Normans who came from France.

The Norman Conquest was the last invasion by another country, but since that time people from all parts of the world have continued to arrive and settle in Britain. Many have come as refugees, fleeing from war, persecution or famine in their own country; some have come hoping to make a better life for themselves.

## The first black people in Britain

The first evidence of black people in Britain dates from Roman times. In the Roman Empire, people from many different countries and ethnic groups served in the Roman army and could become Roman citizens. It is known that there were several high-ranking Africans in the Roman legions and the first Roman emperor who was not a native of Italy was of African descent. The Emperor Septimus Severus came to Britain in 203 AD, keen to consolidate the Roman occupation of the northern territories. When he died, he was cremated (the Roman custom) in York.

There is strong archaeological evidence to suggest that there were other black officers, soldiers and slaves in Britain during the Roman occupation. On Hadrian's Wall – a monumental construction built by the Emperor Hadrian to mark the northern boundary of the empire – there is an inscription that reads: *Numerous Maurorum Aurelianorum*, which can be translated as 'a division of Moors'. Among the skeletons excavated in a Roman cemetery near York, a number show indications of African origins.

## During the years of slavery

The Northamptonshire Pipe Rolls of 1205 mention Peter the Saracen who was a crossbow-maker and a black man. But such records are rare: over 1,000 years following the Roman occupation, there is little in the historical evidence that tells of the presence of black people. However, this is not necessarily an indication that there were none.

Chronologically the next record is of a man employed in the courts of Henry VII and Henry VIII as a musician. Court documents show that in 1507 'John Blanke, the blacke trumpeter' was being paid eight pence a day. Blanke actually means 'white', so it seems probable that this was not his real name, but a nickname bestowed as a joke.

During the sixteenth century, as the slave trade developed and huge numbers of Africans were transported to the Americas and the Caribbean, the total of black people in Britain and Europe increased. Many had arrived with merchants or planters returning to Britain and most were slaves or servants. A smaller number of free black people could also be found in various occupations.

By the end of the sixteenth century, the numbers of black people in Britain had increased dramatically. Among the wealthy it was becoming fashionable to have a black slave, and the court of Queen Elizabeth I included several black musicians. Despite enjoying their entertainment, Elizabeth was not happy about the presence of black people in Britain and frequently declared her views on the subject. During Elizabeth's reign, poverty and all the troubles associated with it were on the increase. Elizabeth decided that black people were part of the problem because they were consuming food that was

Illustration from the Westminster Tournament Roll, 1511

scarce and needed by the poor. The fact that most were not Christians made them all the more unwelcome in protestant England. Elizabeth wrote to the mayors of large cities to complain about the 'blackamoors', instructing that they be deported. Her attempts were unsuccessful.

*Her Majesty understanding that there are of late divers blackamoors brought into this realm, of which kind of people there are already here to manie, considering how God hath blessed this land with great increase of our owne nation ... those kinds of people should be sent forthe of the lande.*

Letter from Queen Elizabeth to city mayors, 1596

*Whereas the Queen's majesty, tendering the good and welfare of her own natural subjects, greatly distressed in these hard times of dearth, is highly discontented to understand the great number of Negroes and blackamoors which (as she is informed) are carried into this realm ... who are fostered and powered here, to the great annoyance of her own liege people that which covet the relief which these people consume ... hath given especial commandment that the said kind of people shall be with all speed avoided and discharged out of this her majesty's realms ...*

Acts of the Privy Council of England, n s XXVI.20–1
Royal Proclamation of 1601

The Duchess of Portsmouth with her servant,
painted in 1682 by Pierre Mignard

Although slavery did not officially end until 1838, the process of gaining emancipation had begun in Britain nearly a century before. Most slaves in Britain in the latter part of the eighteenth century were working as household servants, but their situation was very different from that on the plantations and over the years they had managed to gain a little independence. Black slaves wanted to be treated in the same way as white servants and had successfully demanded wages from their employers. This altered their status: a person in receipt of a wage was treated as a resident of their parish by law, which in turn gave them certain rights. There were also many who ran away, but making a living was extremely hard. In 1731 the mayor of London had decreed that no black people in the city could be taken on as apprentices and so learn a trade.

Thus by the eighteenth century there were significant local populations of black people in several parts of the British Isles, notably London, Manchester, Liverpool, Bristol and Cardiff. The majority were in household service but there were also runaways and free people. It is very difficult to determine the total size of the black population at this time. In a court case relating to a black slave in 1772, a lawyer estimated it to be between 14,000 and 15,000. This rough figure has been generally accepted, although other estimates range between 10,000 and 20,000. What is clear, however, is that in the face of white hostility, the black people began to form distinct communities. In London, for example, black people regularly gathered together for socialising, for mutual support and for music and dancing.

## Black royalty

In eighteenth-century Britain, there is one instance of a person of African descent in more elevated circumstances. Queen Charlotte, the German wife of King George III was the eighth child of Charles Louis Frederick, Prince of Mirow, and a descendant of Margarita de Castro y Sousa, a black branch of the Portuguese Royal House.

From written accounts, it appears that Queen Charlotte had unmistakeably African features, although this is not very apparent in the majority of her portraits. It is almost certain, however, that painters of the time would have deliberately sought to play down the evidence of her ethnic origins in their work. By making her conform to British conventions of beauty and good looks, they would have been more likely to win the favour of their patrons.

Strike while the iron's hot, or 'The consequences of not answering a bell', etching, 1822

Of all the representations by different artists, the portraits by Sir Allan Ramsey had the most distinctively African features.

> Descended from the warlike Vandal race,
> She still preserves that title in her face.
> Tho' shone their triumphs o'er Numidia's plain,
> And Alusian fields their name retain;
> They but subdued the southern world with arms,
> She conquers still with her triumphant charms,
> O! born for rule, – to whose victorious brow
> The greatest monarch of the north must bow.
>
> Poem written on the occasion of the wedding of
> George III and Queen Charlotte

Queen Charlotte is a direct ancestor of the present royal family in Britain. At her coronation, Queen Elizabeth II directly acknowledged both her Asian and African bloodlines.

Queen Charlotte (1744–1818), wife of George III

## The nineteenth century

With the abolition of the slave trade in 1807 and slavery in 1838, the stage appeared to be set for a brighter future for black people in Britain. However, there were other forces at work.

By the beginning of the nineteenth century, natural science had turned to the question of the biological differences between sub-groups of the human race. By observing differences in their physical characteristics, they concluded through various illogical 'scientific' arguments that some ethnic groups were more developed and more intelligent than others. For example, phrenology, one of the fashionable new 'sciences', purported to reveal a person's characteristics by the shape of their skull. Not surprisingly, white people were considered to be a superior race.

> Sir William Lawrence, an eminent surgeon and scientist, drew on the new 'science' of phrenology to reinforce his argument that black people are, by nature, uncivilised.
>
> > [Black people] indulge, almost universally, in disgusting debauchery and sensuality, and display gross selfishness, indifference to the pleasures and pains of others, insensibility to beauty and form, order, and harmony, and an almost entire want of ... elevated sentiments, manly virtues, and moral feeling ... The inferiority of the dark to the white races is much more general and strongly marked in the powers of knowledge and reflection ... I deem the moral and intellectual character of the Negro inferior, and decidedly so, to that of the European.
> >
> > Sir William Lawrence, *Lectures on Physiology, Zoology and the Natural History of Man*, (J. Callow, 1819)

These 'scientific' ideas about the superiority of white (and especially British white) people were taken up by the press, politicians and other influential figures, who used them to justify their actions in building and maintaining the British Empire and their treatment of native people in British colonies all over the world. For British people to rule over the 'inferior' races was somehow a reflection of the natural order of things; black and coloured people could only benefit from serving the more intelligent and civilised white people.

The seeds of racism had been sown during the years when black people were enslaved, and slavery had become associated with skin colour. The anti-slavery society, however, had claimed that black people were equal. The view had been enshrined in their slogan, 'Am I not a man and a brother?' and many thousands had rallied to the cause with sincere intent. But by the latter part of the nineteenth century, the language of race had permeated British society and shaped the British outlook on the rest of the world. So, while black people in Britain were technically free, they were far from being treated as equal.

## Black people in the armed forces

From the seventeenth century onwards, black people were enlisted into the British armed forces. One of the earliest records of a black soldier is that of John Macnell who was born in Antigua in 1744. He is recorded as being enlisted at the age of 12 into the Worcestershire and Sherwood Foresters Regiment.

Regiments were very keen to have black musicians and especially black drummers playing in their bands. Music was an important part of military life: bands accompanied troops into battle and were used to communicate orders. It was generally felt that black people had a natural musical ability, which could be used to advantage.

Throughout the seventeenth and eighteenth centuries, black and white soldiers fought alongside each other. There were black men in many regiments including the Royal Dragoon Guards, the Royal Regiment of Wales, the Princess of Wales Regiment and the Royal Green Jackets. Black and white soldiers were supposedly given the same pay and the same treatment, although some records suggest that black soldiers were not always paid the same. Many black soldiers serving in these regiments were awarded medals for service and bravery.

It was recognised that black men were more likely to survive in wars in foreign countries where as many soldiers were killed by disease as by fighting. In 1794 it was proposed that there should be regiments comprised solely of black soldiers. Thus the West India and East India regiments were formed.

> *I am of opinion that a Corps of one thousand men composed of blacks and Mulattoes, and commanded by British Officers would render more essential service in the Country, than treble this number of Europeans who are unaccustomed to the climate. And as the Enemy have adopted this measure to recruit their armies, I think we should pursue a similar plan to meet them on equal terms.*
>
> Lieutenant-General Sir John Vaughan, 1794

The West India Regiment served in the Caribbean, Central America and West Africa and were awarded many honours.

**MARY SEACOLE** was born Mary Grant in Jamaica in 1805. Her father was a Scottish army officer and her mother a Jamaican mulatto. Mary learned about nursing from her mother who kept a boarding house for invalid soldiers. In 1836 she married Edward Seacole and together they travelled around the Caribbean and Central America. When her husband died, Mary supported herself by nursing in Panama. When she heard about the crisis in the hospitals during the Crimean War, she decided to go and help. In 1854 she travelled to London and applied to the War Office to go to the Crimea as a nurse, but was turned down because she was black. Undeterred, Mary raised funds and travelled to the Crimea by herself.

Mary looked after the sick, tended to the wounded on the battlefield and set up stores where she sold medical supplies. In 1856 she set up a hostel for the injured and convalescent soldiers in Balaclava, using her own money. The soldiers called her 'Mother Seacole'. One soldier wrote in his memoirs:

> *She was a wonderful woman ... all the men swore by her, and in case of any malady, would seek her advice and use her herbal medicines, in preference to reporting themselves to their own doctors. That she did effect some cure is beyond doubt, and her never failing presence amongst the wounded after a battle and assisting them made her beloved by the rank and file of the whole army.*

When the war ended Mary returned to England, ill and destitute. She was saved when the British press publicised her story and well-wishers raised money to pay off her debt. In 1857, she published *The Wonderful Adventures of Mrs Seacole in Many Lands*. The rest of her life was spent working and travelling between London and Kingston. She was awarded the Crimean Medal, the French Legion of Honour and a Turkish medal.

**SAMUEL COLERIDGE-TAYLOR** was the son of a London-trained doctor from Sierra Leone and an English mother. He was born in Holborn in 1875 and lived in Croydon with his mother until the age of 15 years. He went to the Royal College of Music to study the violin but then moved into composing.

In 1903, Coleridge-Taylor was appointed a professor of composition at Trinity College of Music, London. He conducted choirs and orchestras all over England. He was appointed a professor at the Crystal Palace School of Music and Art, and conducted the Bournemouth Symphony Orchestra.

Samuel Coleridge-Taylor was actively involved in Pan-Africanism, a movement that promoted the cause of black people worldwide, emphasising a shared African heritage. With his friend, Duse Mohammed, he founded *The African and Orient Review*, a Pan-Africanist newspaper in London.

Samuel Coleridge-Taylor died in 1912 aged just 37. Although his early works became extremely popular at the time, they were subsequently largely forgotten. Recently, however, there has been renewed interest in his work. His most famous piece, *Hiawatha's Wedding Feast*, was composed when he was 22, and like all his music draws on African, Caribbean and Negro Spiritual traditions.

⊙ Points for reflection

1. Why were black slaves in Britain more successful in resisting their masters than those on the Caribbean plantations?

2. Within the span of a lifetime, British attitudes to black people had apparently shifted from the positive view championed by the anti-slavery movement to the extreme negative views presented by Victorian pseudo-science. What explanations could there be for the apparent change? Why were British people so ready to accept these ideas?

3. What obvious flaws in the racial argument could have been pointed out at the time?

4. Black people appear to have been more readily accepted into the armed forces than into other spheres of life? What might be the reasons for this?

# 13 | Black people in wartime

At the start of the twentieth century Britain had a black population probably in the region of 10,000. Before World War One, the majority of black immigrants had arrived as slaves or servants during the years of slavery or as seamen. The largest black communities in the country comprised black seamen and their families living in the dockside areas of London, Liverpool and Cardiff. There were also a smaller number who had come to work as artists or professional people or to study.

## World War One

At the outbreak of war in 1914, many black people in the British West Indian colonies were very keen to help with the war effort and responded with remarkable loyalty and generosity. They contributed nearly £2 million via the British government and war funds and charities in the UK. They also donated ambulances, aircraft and fuel as well as supplies such as sugar, rum and fruit.

The West India Regiment, having proved their worth in previous campaigns, were keen to fight, but they were kept in the Caribbean until near the end when one of the two battalions was sent to East Africa.

Initially the British government was not keen to have West Indian troops join the fighting, but they were soon forced to change their policy. During the first few months of the war the allied forces suffered heavy losses and in 1915 recruitment in the colonies began. In November 1915, 500 men were sent from Jamaica, with another contingent following in January. The volunteers were drafted into the British West Indies Regiments (completely separate from the West India Regiment) and served in Italy, Palestine and on the Western Front.

The British West Indies Regiment in camp on the Albert, Amiens Road, September 1916

In 1916 the third contingent of Jamaican volunteers left for England on board the ship *Verdala*. There were 25 officers and 1,115 other ranks on board. With the threat of enemy submarines on the route, the ship received orders to change direction and head for Halifax. *Verdala* then ran into a blizzard. Because the ship was inadequately heated and the soldiers had insufficient clothing, five men died on board ship and a further 600 men suffered frostbite which left them permanently debilitated.

The 'Halifax incident' did not help the recruitment campaign in the Caribbean and more aggressive strategies were adopted. Persuasion was largely by means of incentives – glory, the disciplined life, reward of land after the war. As in other countries, the offer was especially attractive to the poor and the unemployed.

The Caribbean volunteers were badly needed by the British forces, but still they were given a guarded reception. Classes as 'aliens', these men could serve in the ranks but were not permitted to become officers.

> *Any person who is for the time being an alien may, if His Majesty think fit to dignify his consent through a Secretary of State, be enlisted in His Majesty's regular forces, so, however, that the number of aliens serving together at any one time in any corps of the regular forces shall not exceed the proportion of one alien to every fifty British subjects, and that an alien so enlisted shall not be capable of holding any higher rank in His Majesty's regular forces than that of a warrant officer or non-commissioned officer.*
>
> The Manual of Military Law

In Britain, black people were suddenly in demand in the munitions factories and to do jobs vacated by those involved in the fighting. By the 1900s, there were more black people employed as seamen than in any other type of work. As war got underway, these men were used in merchant shipping to replace the sailors who had gone to fight in the navy.

By the end of the war, over 16,000 people had been recruited from the West Indies, two-thirds of whom were from Jamaica. The figure includes women, who went mainly into the nursing services. It is estimated that approximately 1,200 of the British West Indies Regiment died, either in fighting or from disease. Those who were rejected or invalided were given little or no support. Having gone to fight for Britain, they were often sent home to the West Indies with no pension, where they would face a poverty-stricken future. Many of the soldiers from the colonies were demobilised in Britain, increasing the black population to approximately 20,000.

## Between the wars

When World War One ended in 1918, the demand for black workers suddenly stopped. The situation was particularly bad for black seamen. Shipping companies chose to employ white sailors now that they were available, leaving hundreds of black seamen out of work. Black people – who had supported Britain during the crisis – found themselves not only out of work but also disadvantaged because of blatant discrimination. The situation became increasingly volatile and in 1919 a number of British ports, notably Tyneside, Liverpool and Cardiff, became the scene of race riots.

Following the rioting, white seamen's unions lobbied against employment of 'coloured aliens', which led to The Aliens Order of 1920, and the Special Restriction (Coloured Alien Seamen) Order of 1925. Now it was even more difficult for black people to find employment. In the years between the wars, discrimination and animosity built up and black people faced the 'colour bar' in all areas of life.

## World War Two

Up until the start of World War Two, a colour bar in the armed forces meant that no black people could join up, but in 1939 the government relaxed the ruling and the recruitment campaign was extended across the countries of the Commonwealth.

### The British colonies involved in the war

**Africa**
Anglo-Egyptian Sudan
Basutoland
Bechuanaland
British East Africa (Kenya)
British Gold Coast
British Somaliland
Egypt
Gambia
Nigeria
Northern Rhodesia
Nyasaland
Sierra Leone
South Africa
Southern Rhodesia
Uganda and Zanzibar

**Atlantic Islands**
Ascension
Sandwich Islands
South Georgia
St. helena
Tristan da Cunha

**Australasia and Pacific Ocean**
Antipodes
Auckland
Australia
Borneo
Bounty
Campbell
Chatham Islands
Christmas
Cook Islands
Ducie
Elice Islands
Fanning
Flint
Fiji Islands
Gilbert Islands
Kermadec Islands
Macquarie
Malden
New Guinea
New Hebrides
New Zealand
Norfolk
Palmyra
Pitcairn
Pheonix Islands

Solomon Islands
Tokelau Islands
Tonga

**America**
Canada
Falkland Islands

**Asia**
Singapore

**Europe**
Cyprus
Great Britain
Malta

**Indian Empire**
Aden
Burma
Ceylon
India

**Indian Ocean Islands**
Andaman Islands
Cocos Islands
Mauritius
Nicobar Islands
Seychelles

**Middle East**
Arabia (protectorates)
Kuwait
Oman
Newfoundland

**West Indies**
Bahamas
Barbados
British Guiana
British Honduras
Grenada
Jamaica
Leeward Islands
St. Lucia
St. Vincent
Trinidad and Tobago

According to Imperial War Museum records, around 7,000 West Indians were recruited into the British forces. Of these, nearly 6,000 were in the RAF; most worked as skilled technicians and ground crew in the bases but 300 served as aircrew, with nearly a third of those eventually receiving military honours. In the army, some West Indians joined the Royal Engineers in 1941, but it was not until 1944 that a Caribbean Regiment was formed. The regiment of 1,000 men was trained in Europe but did not see active service.

Around 600 women from the West Indies joined the Auxiliary Territorial Service (ATS). Of these, about 200 went to the USA and 100 to Britain, while the rest remained in the Caribbean. Over 80 West Indian women served in the Women's Auxiliary Air Force in the UK.

**HAROLD MOODY** was born in Kingston, Jamaica, in 1882. In 1904 he went to Britain to study medicine at King's College, London. After qualifying as a doctor, he found himself refused hospital jobs and accommodation because he was black. In 1913 he set up his own medical practice in Peckham (south-east London) which became very successful. Shortly afterwards he married an English nurse whom he had met when he was a medical student.

Moody was a tireless campaigner for black people. He formed a non-radical group called 'The League of Coloured Peoples' to fight for justice and equality for Caribbean and African people. They took the case of sacked seamen to parliament, defended people in court, raised money to help hundreds of destitute black children and found work for the unemployed. At the start of World War Two, Harold Moody argued for equality for all service people, European and non-European alike.

Thousands more Caribbean people were employed to maintain the infrastructures such as the health service, public transport and armaments, and West Indian seamen once again took jobs in the Merchant Navy, as in World War One. Many black people also volunteered for civil defence, working as air-raid wardens, auxiliary firefighters, first-aid workers and mobile canteen staff.

There was no fighting on the Caribbean islands, but the area came under direct threat as German submarines were sent to destroy ships carrying oil and bauxite to the USA and the UK. Five British colonies became outposts of defence against German submarines.

In 1942, the arrival in Britain of thousands of American servicemen created a particular problem. In the American forces, black and white soldiers were completely segregated – so how should British people treat black American servicemen? The debate eventually reached parliament and it was decided that Britain should fall into line with the American approach. The official advice was to avoid mixing with coloured troops, where possible.

West Indian troops suffered as a result of this imported racism. By 1942 there were 8,000 of them in Britain and they frequently found themselves persecuted by white American soldiers.

Sergeant L. Lynch, an RAF serviceman who won the
Air Gunner's Trophy in 1943 and 1944

ATS recruits from the West Indies

Alvin Christie from Kingston, Jamaica, working in a tank factory in the north of England

> *During that period, as far as we were concerned, the motto was 'kill or be killed', and we didn't mean the enemy ... I have never laid a hand on a German or Italian soldier, who was supposed to be the enemy, but I had to fight or run like hell to save my skin when confronted by the so-called allies.*
>
> Stanley Hodges relating his off-duty experiences as a Caribbean airman in England, from *Lest We Forget, The Experiences of World War II West Indian Ex-Service Personnel*, Robert N. Murray, Hansib, 1996

---

### ☉ Points for reflection

1. Why did so many people from the British colonies volunteer for the British forces in the World Wars? Why would they want to support Britain in this way?

2. What could have been the reasons for British government's decision to conform to the American way of treating black soldiers in World War Two?

---

### ●→ Find out more

What were the main causes of the race riots between the wars? Who was involved? What were the catalysts for violence?

---

# 14

# Post-war migrants and settlers

After World War Two, with its position as an international power weakened, Britain began to retreat from some of its territories abroad. The first withdrawal took place in India. Such a large country in which there was a great deal of unrest was becoming increasingly difficult to govern, and in 1947 India gained independence. This was followed by decolonisation in West African and West Indian countries. To maintain links with its former colonies, the British Commonwealth of Nations (generally known as the 'Commonwealth') was formed.

| Colonial name | Modern name | British rule began | Independence gained |
|---|---|---|---|
| Anguilla | Anguilla | 1650 | Dep. |
| Antigua | Antigua and Barbuda | 1632 | 1981 |
| Barbados | Barbados | 1625 | 1966 |
| British Virgin Islands | British Virgin Islands | 1672 | Dep. |
| Cayman Islands | Cayman Islands | 1670 | Dep. |
| Dominica | Dominica | 1761 | 1978 |
| Grenada | Grenada | 1762 | 1974 |
| Jamaica | Jamaica | 1655 | 1962 |
| Montserrat | Montserrat | 1633 | Dep. |
| St Christopher, Nevis | St Kitts and Nevis | 1624 | 1983 |
| St Lucia | St Lucia | 1664 | 1979 |
| St Vincent | St Vincent and The Grenadines | 1762 | 1979 |
| Tobago | Trinidad and Tobago | 1763 | 1962 |
| Trinidad | Trinidad and Tobago | 1797 | 1962 |
| Turks and Caicos Islands | Turks and Caicos Islands | 1678 | Dep. |

(Dep. = remains a UK-dependent territory)

## Post-war immigration

After World War Two, the British government was faced with a shortage of labour and began to recruit workers from abroad. In the years immediately after the war, people came from all over Europe: Hungarians, Italians, Poles and Irish arrived in large numbers. In 1948 the nationality act conferred citizenship on all subjects in British colonies and on citizens of the newly-created Commonwealth countries, which made it easier for the government to recruit from the Caribbean and from the Indian subcontinent.

Life for many people in the West Indies after the war was extremely hard. The cost of living had doubled, wages were low, the level of unemployment was high and social security benefits were non-existent. Those without jobs were desperate. It was therefore not surprising that many chose to respond to posters proclaiming 'Britain needs hands' and seek work in 'The Mother Country'.

While people in the Caribbean did see Britain as a source of oppression, they also thought of themselves as British citizens and as part of an international colonial system. It has been widely believed that these people travelled in search of a utopian dream, believing in 'streets paved with gold'. In fact they were not completely naive, having been partly acquainted with the reality from islanders who had been to Britain and returned home. Their eagerness was not born out of illusion so much as from being used to the idea of travelling to find employment – and the prospects in Britain looked better than the ones at home.

## A welcome for *Empire Windrush*

On 22 June 1948, a former British military ship, MV *Empire Windrush*, docked at Tilbury, England. It had sailed from Trinidad, Kingston, Tampico, Havana and Bermuda. On board were British people, immigrants from Poland who had travelled via Mexico and wanted to settle in Britain, two stowaways and 492 Jamaicans. Many of the Jamaicans had served with the Allied Forces during the war and these first arrivals were given an enthusiastic welcome. The *London Evening Standard* had the headline 'Welcome home'. The arrival of *Empire Windrush* became a symbolic event, marking the start of a period of immigration that would last for 14 years.

P.M. 23

Name of Ship ___ M.V. "EMPIRE WINDRUSH" ___ . Port of Arrival _____ . Date of Arrival ____ 19__

Steamship Line ___ THE NEW ZEALAND SHIPPING CO.LTD. ___ . Whence Arrived TRINIDAD, KINGSTON, TAMPICO, HAVANA AND BERMUDA.

NAMES AND DESCRIPTIONS OF **BRITISH** PASSENGERS.

The list of passengers on board the *Empire Windrush*

For the first few years, the numbers crossing the Atlantic were relatively small. In October 1948, 180 West Indians arrived on the *Orbita*, followed by 39 Jamaicans on the *Reine del Pacifico*. Then in 1952, legislation in the USA restricted immigration from the Caribbean. The possibility of similar legislation in Britain meant that the door might not be open for ever; the prospect of not being able to leave probably prompted many people into a decision.

| Year | Number of Caribbean immigrants (approximate) |
|------|----------------------------------------------|
| 1949 | 252 |
| 1950 | below 1,000 |
| 1951 | 1,000 |
| 1952 | 2,000 |
| 1953 | 2,000 |
| 1954 | 10,000 |
| 1955 | 24,473 |
| 1956 | 26,441 |
| 1957 | 22,473 |
| 1958 | 16,511 |

By 1961 the number of immigrants had increased to over 66,000 a year. Between 1951 and 1961 between 230,000 and 280,000 people with British passports left the Caribbean for Britain.

A small number of migrants who were recruited by London Transport or by the new health service had their passage paid for. The majority, however, had to find a fare of up to £85. To begin with most of the migrants were men, but once they became established in Britain they began to bring their wives and families over to join them.

Passengers from the *Empire Windrush* at Tilbury, England, 1948

The passage to Britain took about two weeks. The accommodation on board ship was fairly basic but adequate.

> When the Morrison family arrived in March 1962, it made the front-page news in The Birmingham Post. Mr Morrison was already in the UK and he set out from Smethwick in the West Midlands to meet his family at Southampton. He missed them, but thanks to the kindness of some taxi drivers, Mrs Morrison and her children were driven to their new home. Many readers of the newspaper thought the family was destitute and began sending clothes, toys and other goods to help them.

## Settling in Britain

After arriving at the docks, the immigrants were taken by train to their destination. Most of them went to London and the rest were dispersed to other industrial cities including Liverpool, Manchester, Birmingham, Bristol, Leeds, Bradford, Nottingham and Leicester.

In London and other large cities, wartime bombing had resulted in housing shortages. Many people were accommodated in 'temporary' pre-fabricated houses (known as prefabs) and many were still living in them decades later. With no local authority housing available, finding homes for the immigrants presented difficulties. Many of the first arrivals were accommodated in hostels and temporary camps. One group of 236 people was housed in a deep air-raid shelter under Clapham Common in London.

At home in London, 1950s

Finding rented property was difficult because of racial discrimination on the part of landlords. It was not uncommon to see property for rent with signs that stated 'no blacks' or 'no coloureds'. If a room could be found, the rent would be approximately £2.50 a week – about half a person's wages. For that they could expect cramped, unhygienic accommodation. Up to six men or six women might share a room, often taking it in turns to sleep in the available beds. In many rented houses there were no proper kitchen facilities – just a stove on the landing – because the owners of the house kept the kitchen for their personal use. Often two or three families would pool their resources so that they could buy one house between them. Again, conditions would be crowded and they might have to take it in turns to sleep in the beds available.

For the Caribbean immigrants, Britain was a strange country full of un-familiar sights and experiences. Unaccustomed to seeing brick-built terraced houses and puzzled by the smoke coming out of the top, many assumed they were some sort of factory. One arrival, Joseph Lewis, later reported that initially he had been fearful of the white people and had planned to return to Jamaica as fast as he could. Forty years later, he was still in England.

Despite warnings about the climate, the cold temperatures still came as a shock. Victor Dyer was a skilled carpenter from Clarendon, Jamaica, who arrived in Britain in 1961. He went to work on a building site but was not wearing enough clothes. He eventually fainted from hypothermia and ended up in the hospital.

Most of the people who arrived were skilled workers in their twenties. (Only 13 per cent of men and 5 per cent of women had no skills.) However, few ended up with work that suited their skills and experience. Many were disappointed to find themselves doing low-status jobs – the ones white people did not want. These jobs were mainly in the construction industry, hospitals, transport, nursing and cleaning.

## Facing antagonism

Although the very first Caribbean post-war immigrants were given a warm welcome as war veterans and as workers who would help solve the labour problem, this was sadly not indicative of what most immigrants were later to experience as they tried to make a new life for themselves.

Among the white British population, negative attitudes to black people ran

## Georgia's story

Georgia was 14 years old when she reluctantly left Jamaica in 1962. She did not mind the idea of visiting Britain, but did not want to live there. She was very homesick. She describes her first impressions of the country: '… factories, factories all around. They couldn't be houses, there were no flowers in the gardens like where I had come from. And I wondered where the houses were.' What she knew about Britain before travelling came largely from Christmas cards, so she expected snow, robins and bright, sunny weather. She was disappointed to find it was mostly dull and grey.

British food seemed bland and tasteless. 'The bread was awful,' she says. 'It just tasted nasty, but it's better now.' There was also a degree of culture shock. Georgia was not used to the amount of cosmetics and make-up that young girls were using. To her, they seemed to be very sexually aware. 'I was surprised with the lack of modesty in fellow female students,' she explains. She remembers not being allowed to watch *Coronation Street* because it was after 7.30 pm. 'Also,' she says, 'we were not allowed to watch anything with kissing in it.'

And she found other differences between British and Caribbean cultures: 'I couldn't see why people couldn't give out of love, rather than giving to get and not with a willing spirit. Giving with strings attached was a totally new phenomenon.'

Georgia was aware of overt racism in the school she attended. Fortunately, she was good at sports and could win trophies, so the other pupils accepted her. But she remembers the teachers' prejudice: 'They clearly lacked understanding of people from the Caribbean. Their expectation of us was not very high, so they did not give you anything challenging to do at school, and put you in remedial classes.'

from a general lack of regard and a vague discomfort to overt hostility. There was a widespread feeling that black people were ignorant, uneducated, uncivilised heathens who spoke strange languages, ate odd food and carried nasty diseases. For many whites, black people were objects of fear and resentment.

As a result of deep-seated prejudice among the white British population, black people found it difficult to get jobs and housing. They were shunned by white workmates and neighbours who wanted no contact with these 'intruders'.

Finding themselves unwelcome in pubs and other public meeting places, black people formed their own social gatherings, which included the blues clubs. Even the churches did not welcome black faces in their congregations. The nonconformist missionaries that had gone to the Caribbean during the slavery years had a significant effect on the island of Jamaica, yet those same churches were not keen to accept black people when they turned up at church in Britain. As a result, black Christians formed their own churches, usually holding lively meetings with African-influenced worship, much as they had done in the Caribbean.

By the late 1950s, the antagonism that had been simmering for nearly a decade started to boil over. In 1958, riots, fighting and vicious racial attacks erupted in Nottingham. Just two weeks later there were similar scenes in London's Notting Hill.

> *People talk about a colour problem arising in Britain. How can there be a colour problem here? Even after all the immigration of the past few years, there are only 190,000 coloured people in our population of over 50 million – that is, only four out of every 1,000. The real problem is not black skins, but white prejudice.*
>
> Tom Driberg, Labour Party Chairman,
> speaking at the Trades Union Congress
>
> Report of the Proceedings at the 90th Annual Trades Union Congress, 1958

## Staunching the flow

After the 1958 riots, racist attacks on black people continued. Race relations and immigration became the subject of heated national debate and a key political issue. All political parties were anxious to be seen to be addressing the problem. But the 'problem', as they now saw it, was the presence of black people in Britain – and the more black people, the greater the

## Levi's story

By the age of 28, Levi had risen to a high level in the police force in Kingston, Jamaica. He thought he knew quite a lot about England: 'We had the radio and it kept advertising, "Come to Britain, Britain Needs You". I thought of it as the Mother Country and England had ruled it (Jamaica) for over 300 years. All in the country is based on Britain, with a statue of Queen Victoria in Kingston and some Generals. As a black person I had known all along about the English.' Encouraged by his friends, he travelled over to Britain in 1963.

Levi was shocked to find that the only work he could obtain was in a factory earning £9 a week. He also had difficulty finding somewhere to live, and his life in Britain stood in stark contrast to the one he had had in Jamaica, where he had enjoyed a high standard of living: 'We were comfortable before we came.'

Levi's reactions to the reality of life in Britain were mixed. He was impressed by London, but couldn't believe some of the sights: 'In Jamaica we don't have houses joined, I thought they were barracks, like slaves used to live in.' He also found the weather disappointing: 'The first time I saw snow, I just couldn't believe it. In Jamaica it's one weather all year round. In the end, I couldn't say I enjoyed it, but you get accustomed to it.'

Overall, he was disappointed because he thought 'things would be more glorious.' He found the British people 'scornful and resentful – you felt it especially if you sat next to them on the bus.'

problem. As a result, legislation was passed that effectively staunched the inflow of black people into the country. The Commonwealth Immigrants Act 1962, restricted admission of Commonwealth settlers to those who had been issued with employment vouchers. Entry control was established and conviction of an offence within five years of arrival would automatically lead to deportation.

> *The immigrants are hurrying to beat the Immigration Bill which will probably become law about Easter.*
>
> *The Birmingham Post*, Friday, 23 March, 1962

Subsequent new arrivals were comparatively few and almost all had family already living in Britain. During the 1960s and early 1970s, a series of bills was passed that aimed to tighten immigration control further. The Immigration Act 1971 virtually ended all black immigration; at the same time repatriation was encouraged and tough measures against illegal immigrants were brought in.

### ⊙ Points for reflection

1. Why do you think people in the Caribbean saw Britain as the 'Mother Country'?

2. What emotions would the passengers on board the ships bound for Britain feel?

3. How did the experience of the journey and new land for post-war immigrants compare with that of the slaves taken from Africa?

4. The post-war immigrants faced discrimination and racial prejudice in all areas of life. On what was it based? How had people in twentieth-century Britain acquired these attitudes to black people?

### ●→ Find out more

What other forms did discrimination and prejudice against black people take? How did black people respond?

# 15

# Born black, born British

Immediately after World War Two, black people in Britain numbered only a few thousand. By the time of the 1971 census, when virtually all immigration of non-whites had ceased, there were an estimated 529,000 people of West Indian descent. But whereas the first few arrivals had been welcomed as war comrades, coming to lend support in a post-war labour shortage, black immigrants were now seen as a problem. The Immigration Acts of the 1960s and 1970s were discriminatory – imposing different controls on black and white citizens of the Commonwealth – and this only served to reinforce the view that black people were a source of trouble.

At the same time as trying to limit the growth of the black population, the government had attempted to address the problem of discrimination in British society. The 1965 Race Relations Act outlawed the 'colour bar' – the common practice of banning black and coloured people from using public services or entering public places.

A further Race Relations Act in 1968 made it illegal to refuse housing, employment or public services to people because of their ethnic background. However, the Act exempted national services, such as the police, from legal proceedings, and the Opposition MP Quintin Hogg observed that it was unfair to treat private employers one way and public employers another.

The Act also set up two new organisations: the Race Relations Board, to deal with complaints of discrimination, and the Community Relations Commission, to promote 'harmonious community relations'.

## 'Rivers of Blood'

Race issues were forced to the top of the political agenda following a speech on 22 April 1968 by the right-wing Conservative MP, Enoch Powell. In what has become known as the 'Rivers of Blood' speech, he spoke against immigration into Britain from Commonwealth countries, warning against the threat posed to the nation by coloured people. He spoke of the nation 'busily engaged in heaping up its own funeral pyre'. His blatantly racist remarks caused outrage among MPs, and he was sacked from the shadow cabinet soon afterwards. The government was even more shocked, however, at the strength of reaction the speech provoked in some quarters. Some sections of the media applauded it, while thousands of workers staged strikes in protest and marched to Downing Street in support of Enoch Powell.

Some black people felt that Enoch Powell had stirred up trouble and created barriers that had not been there previously. Others felt that the barriers had always been present, but the speech had given those with racist views a platform and an opportunity to verbalise their racism.

## A new generation

By the 1970s, two fifths of black people in Britain had been born here. They were not immigrants, but like their parents, they still faced prejudice and discrimination.

Four political and economic planning reports published between 1974 and 1976 described some of the problems faced by people of Caribbean and Asian descent. They found that black people were:

- more likely to be in overcrowded housing (this affected 40 per cent of black people compared with 11 per cent of white)
- more frequently rejected for jobs without being told the real reason
- more likely to be unemployed (between 1973 and 1976, the increase in unemployment among black people was double that for the population as a whole)
- more likely to be doing work below the level of their skills and capabilities.

The situation in education was similarly bleak. One study (David Kirp, 1979) found that children of West Indian parents were three to four times more likely to be classed as 'educationally subnormal'. The problem was not

so much overt discrimination on the part of teachers as the fact that they were subconsciously lowering their expectations of black children – and treating them accordingly.

Set against this backdrop of general prejudice was the continuation of racial violence across the country and the accumulating evidence of police brutality towards members of the black community, especially young black men. The scourge of institutional racism was becoming a national issue.

In 1976, the government set up the Commission for Racial Equality (CRE) to try and tackle some of the problems. The Commission was given the power to force companies and other bodies to comply with the 1968 Race Relations Act – which was not being universally enforced. The manager of one Birmingham night club ordered to lift its race ban told the BBC that he had to limit the numbers of ethnic minorities in his club to preserve a 'happy situation' and to avoid aggressive confrontations. 'We'll operate as we have done for the last 10 years – I think we have to limit all sorts of people and coloured people fit into that category,' he said.

## Riots and unrest

But the unrest continued, and in 1981 racial hostility reached a new level. The trouble was sparked off when 13 black people died in a house fire in Deptford, but police would not consider the possibility that it was a racial attack. In response, 15,000 people staged a protest march, demanding justice

Brixton riots, 1981

for black people. When, one month later, police mounted 'Operation Swamp' to combat crime in Brixton, London, black people saw this as police retaliation and were resentful that many young black men seemed to be unfairly stopped and searched and bullied by officers. In July 1981, rioting broke out in Brixton, quickly spreading to Toxteth in Liverpool, and then to many other cities in Britain. Young black people fought against the police, held areas under siege and burnt down buildings. The nation was shocked and appalled at the scale and intensity of the violence.

An inquiry was held, and in November 1981 Lord Scarman's report described the riots as the worst outbreak of disorder in the UK that century, blaming 'racial disadvantage that is a fact of British life'. Scarman recognised that much of the widespread unrest had its roots in social and economic deprivation and in racial discrimination. Following the Scarman report, major changes were implemented in policing, including the setting up of the Police Complaints Authority, and an end to the hated 'Sus' law, which allowed officers to arrest anyone they suspected of loitering with intent. Lord Scarman called for a new emphasis on community policing and said more people from ethnic minorities should be recruited into the force. The findings of the report led to the introduction of many measures to improve trust and understanding between the police and ethnic minority communities.

In 1985 rioting broke out again in Brixton after a black woman (the mother of a wanted man) was accidentally shot and wounded during a police raid on her home. Further unrest followed in several cities and riots erupted once again in Toxteth in Liverpool and Peckham in London.

## A defining moment

In the 1990s, racist violence continued: in 1996, the British Crime Survey reported that an estimated 200,000 black and Asian people had suffered racial attack or harassment the previous year.

On 22 April 1993, black teenager Stephen Lawrence was murdered by five white youths in what was undoubtedly an unprovoked, racially motivated attack. No one has ever been convicted of his murder. Stephen was by no means the only victim of a racial attack, but his death and the subsequent mishandling of the murder investigation by the Metropolitan Police became an almost iconic event in the battle against institutional racism. The 'Stephen Lawrence Inquiry' resulted in the publication in 1999 of the Macpherson Report – an event that has since been described as a 'defining moment in British race relations'.

The report condemned incompetence and racism in the police force and made 70 recommendations aimed at stamping out institutional racism within the force and in wider society.

> *If racism is to be eliminated from our society there must be a co-ordinated effort to prevent its growth. This needs to go well beyond the police services.*
>
> *It is incumbent upon every institution to examine their policies and practices to guard against disadvantaging any section of our communities.*
>
> Macpherson Report

The government accepted the charges, and responded by amending and extending existing legislation. The Race Relations (Amendment) Act 2000 makes it unlawful for public authorities to discriminate in the exercise of their functions and to discriminate against anyone on the grounds of race, colour, nationality (including citizenship), or ethnic or national origin. The Act also imposes positive duties on many public authorities to promote race equality.

## Overcoming prejudice

The picture of life for black people in Britain in the second half of the twentieth century was fairly bleak. These people – many of them descendants of African slaves – may have enjoyed a kind of freedom denied to their ancestors, but they have not enjoyed the same acceptance, opportunity or justice as their white neighbours.

However, there are many black men and women who have overcome discrimination and prejudice to enjoy success in their careers and acceptance in their communities. There are also those whose achievements have become widely known and who have made a significant contribution to society. Black people have been particularly prominent in music and sport, but there are influential black figures in many different fields. Just a few of these are mentioned overleaf – not as tokens, but as a small indication of the range and quality of contribution made by black people; it is not within the scope of this book to provide a comprehensive list of the many who could have been included.

## Music

Western pop has been influenced at all stages of its development by black American music. The roots of black influence go back to the 'spirituals' and work songs of the African slaves. In the nineteenth century, black music was fundamental to the development of ragtime and blues music, and in the early twentieth century, in the development of jazz. In the 1960s, a style of Jamaican music known as ska became very popular on both sides of the Atlantic. Also from Jamaica came rock steady and then reggae, both of which evolved from ska. Since the 1960s, many other popular styles have emerged that owe something to black music: rock, funk, rhythm and blues, rap, hip-hop and techno.

**JOAN ARMATRADING** was born in St Kitts in 1950 and moved to the UK with her family in 1958. She rose to fame in the 1970s and her music has influenced many contemporary female artists.

**JAZZIE B** is a DJ, music producer and entrepreneur whose record company, Soul II Soul helped to create a new distinctive black British music sound.

**ERROL BROWN,** singer and songwriter was born in Jamaica and moved to Britain aged 12. He fronted the 1970s' band Hot Chocolate. He has since had success as a solo artist and in 2003 was awarded an MBE for services to popular music.

**SEAL** was one of the most popular singers in the 1990s. His blend of soul, dance and rock brought him chart hits on both sides of the Atlantic.

There are also black people in the world of classical and jazz music.

**WAYNE MARSHALL** is a pianist, organist and conductor of international reputation.

**COURTNEY PINE** is one of Britain's leading jazz saxophonists. He has done much to develop and popularise British jazz, and his tracks have made the top 40 in the charts.

## Arts and media

**ZADIE SMITH** was born in London in 1975 to an English father and a Jamaican mother. She won wide acclaim with her debut novel, *White Teeth*, and is now regarded as one of Britain's most talented young novelists.

**BENJAMIN ZEPHANIAH** was born in Birmingham but spent some of his childhood in Jamaica. His distinctive Jamaican-influenced poetry has been widely published and performed; he is known both as a poet and as a social commentator.

In the past, black people have suffered from being misrepresented in the media and advertising through negative or stereotyped images – when they were represented at all. More recently, black people have been prominent in the public eye as actors, TV presenters and journalists – as well as working 'behind the scenes'. Black people have also been used to present positive images in advertising. Howard Brown, for example, was chosen from staff at the Halifax Bank and has become the well-liked 'face' of the organisation.

**NAOMI CAMPBELL** was born in 1970 in Streatham. She became the first black woman to appear on the cover of *Time* and *Vogue* in England and America and has enjoyed international fame as a 'supermodel'.

**LENNY HENRY** was born in Dudley, West Midlands to a Jamaican family. He is an actor and a comedian as well as one of the founding members of Comic Relief that has helped to raise millions of pounds over the years for good causes. He is also active in promoting young black performers and multi-ethnic programming.

**SIR TREVOR MACDONALD** was born in Trinidad in 1939 and has had a distinguished career in journalism and broadcasting. He has become known as the 'face' of ITN news after years of fronting its flagship 'News at Ten' bulletin.

## Sport

**JOHN BARNES** was born in Kingston, Jamaica in 1963. He became an international footballer and now works as an ambassador for Save the Children.

**LINFORD CHRISTIE** was born in Jamaica in 1960. He was Britain's most successful sprinter and became the first track athlete ever to hold the world, Olympic, European and Commonwealth titles at the same time.

**COLIN JACKSON** is of Jamaican descent and was born in Cardiff in 1967. He is one of the best athletes in the history of British and Welsh athletics and holder of two world records – indoor 60m hurdles and outdoor 110m hurdles. He was awarded the MBE in 1990 for his services to athletics.

**LENNOX LEWIS** was born in 1965 in London. He is the second boxer in 100 years to hold three boxing belts, the IBF, WBA and WBC. Lennox was awarded an honorary doctorate by the University of North London for his services to sports and his support in the community for the education of disadvantaged young people.

**TESSA SANDERSON,** a javelin thrower and television personality, was the first British woman to win a throwing event in the Olympics.

**DALEY THOMPSON** was an outstanding British athlete who not only won the Olympic decathalon title twice but raised the profile and level of performance of the whole event. He was awarded the CBE in 2000.

**IAN WRIGHT** was born in 1963 in Woolwich. He was not the first black footballer to play for Britain but he has made a place for himself in the hearts of the British people, through his personality and his work on television. His contribution to football was recognised with an MBE.

## Political and public life

**DIANE ABBOTT** was born in 1953 in London and became the first black MP. Diane has done much to raise the issue of British– Caribbean children's underachieving in Britain, and other race equality issues.

**BARONESS AMOS** was born in Guyana in 1954 and was the first black woman cabinet minister (she is currently the Secretary of State for International Development) and joint first black woman peer. She became Leader of the House of Lords.

**MIKE FULLER** was born in 1960 and began his career as a cadet in the Metropolitan Police before joining the Special Branch. He later joined the Met's racist and violent crime offences force after the Met was accused of 'institutional racism' in the Macpherson Report. He subsequently became Britain's first black Chief Constable.

**SIR BILL MORRIS** was born in Bombay, Jamaica in 1938 and came to Britain in 1954 when he joined his recently widowed mother in Britain, living in the Handsworth district of Birmingham. He was elected General Secretary of the Transport and General Workers Union in 1991 and re-elected to this highly influential post in 1995. He has also contributed to public life through service on numerous advisory boards and committees.

## Looking to the future

The 2001 census numbered the population of Britain at over 58 million, with over 1.1 million describing themselves as 'black'. Of this group of Caribbean or African (not Asian) descent, more than half have been born in the British Isles.

| Ethnic group | Total population count | Percentage of total population | Percentage of minority ethnic population |
|---|---|---|---|
| White | 54,153,898 | 92.1 | n/a |
| Black Caribbean | 565,876 | 1.0 | 12.2 |
| Black African | 485,277 | 0.8 | 10.5 |
| Black other | 97,585 | 0.2 | 2.1 |

UK population by ethnic group, from Census 2001

How do these black British people now see themselves? What sort of society do they now find themselves in? Certainly, we have come a long way since the days of slavery and when black people were deemed by 'scientists' to be biologically inferior. Certainly, the laws of the country are finally being changed to ensure justice for all, regardless of racial origins. Certainly, there is evidence of a society and a culture that is beginning to embrace the contribution made by black people (and by other ethnic minorities). And compared with many other countries, Britain provides a positive model of a multi-cultural society, where ethnic diversity is not only tolerated, but welcomed as something that enriches life for everyone.

Yet there is still no room for complacency. In 2003, a major study commissioned by the BBC indicated that most people of all races thought that while Britain was a more tolerant society than a decade ago, more than half believe it is still a racist society. Years of prejudice and discrimination have left their mark on our society, and racial barriers are still in evidence.

---

### ⊙ Points for reflection

1. Why did Enoch Powell's speech in 1968 produce so much unexpected support?

2. What factors contributed to the continuation of racist violence in the 1980s and 1990s?

3. David Kirp's study in 1979 found that teachers were more likely to regard children of Caribbean descent as 'educationally subnormal'. Why do you think these children – more than any other ethnic group – were likely to be seen in this way? What would be the likely long-term consequences for these children?

4. What other ethnic groups have suffered persecution or discrimination – either in Britain or in other countries? What are the causes? In what ways is it similar to the experiences of black people in Britain, and in what ways is it different?

5. Do you think that their ancestors' experience of slavery (see Chapters 5–7) and of immigration (see Chapter 14) would have any effect on people of Caribbean origin in Britain today, and if so what?

6. What can we learn from the interconnected history of British, African and Caribbean peoples?

---

●→ **Find out more**

Research the part played by black culture in the development of pop music.
Find out more about the contribution made by black people to British sport.
Research the life and achievements of a black Briton alive today.

# Timeline

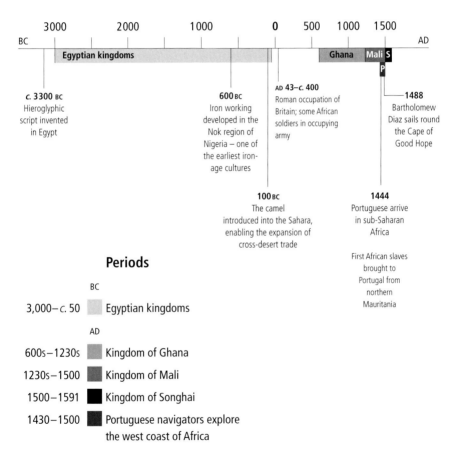

| | | | | | | |
|---|---|---|---|---|---|---|
| 3000 | 2000 | 1000 | 0 | 500 | 1000 | 1500 |
| BC | | | | | | AD |

Egyptian kingdoms · Ghana · Mali · S · P

**c. 3300 BC**
Hieroglyphic
script invented
in Egypt

**600 BC**
Iron working
developed in the
Nok region of
Nigeria – one of
the earliest iron-
age cultures

**AD 43–c. 400**
Roman occupation of
Britain; some African
soldiers in occupying
army

**1488**
Bartholomew
Diaz sails round
the Cape of
Good Hope

**100 BC**
The camel
introduced into the Sahara,
enabling the expansion of
cross-desert trade

**1444**
Portuguese arrive
in sub-Saharan
Africa

First African slaves
brought to
Portugal from
northern
Mauritania

## Periods

BC

3,000– c. 50 — Egyptian kingdoms

AD

600s–1230s — Kingdom of Ghana

1230s–1500 — Kingdom of Mali

1500–1591 — Kingdom of Songhai

1430–1500 — Portuguese navigators explore
the west coast of Africa

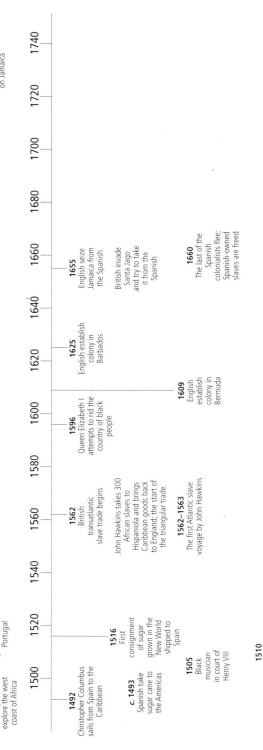

**1430–1500**
Portuguese navigators explore the west coast of Africa

**1500s**
Arabs bring sugar to Spain and Portugal

**1720–1739**
First Maroon War on Jamaica

**1492**
Christopher Columbus sails from Spain to the Caribbean

**c. 1493**
Spanish take sugar cane to the Americas

**1516**
First consignment of sugar grown in the New World shipped to Spain

**1505**
Black musician in court of Henry VIII

**1510**
50 African slaves taken to work in gold mines of Hispaniola

**1518**
4,000 African slaves taken to work in Spanish colonies

**1562**
British transatlantic slave trade begins

John Hawkins takes 300 African slaves to Hispaniola and brings Caribbean goods back to England; the start of the triangular trade.

**1562–1563**
The first Atlantic slave voyage by John Hawkins

**1596**
Queen Elizabeth I attempts to rid the country of black people

**1609**
English establish colony in Bermuda

**1625**
English establish colony in Barbados

**1655**
English seize Jamaica from the Spanish

British invade Santa Jago and try to take it from the Spanish

**1660**
The last of the Spanish colonialists flee; Spanish-owned slaves are freed

**1670**
Approximately 900 sugar plantations on the British settlement in Barbados

**1672**
Royal African Company founded to control British slave trade

1500    1520    1540    1560    1580    1600    1620    1640    1660    1680    1700    1720    1740

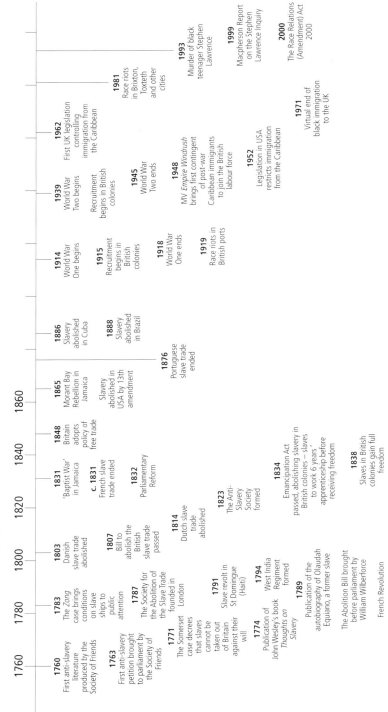

**1795–1796**
Second Maroon War on Jamaica

**1760**
First anti-slavery literature produced by the Society of Friends

**1763**
First anti-slavery petition brought to parliament by the Society of Friends

**1771**
The Somerset case decrees that slaves cannot be taken out of Britain against their will

**1774**
Publication of John Wesley's book *Thoughts on Slavery*

**1783**
The *Zong* case brings conditions on slave ships to public attention

**1787**
The Society for the Abolition of the Slave Trade founded in London

**1789**
Publication of the autobiography of Olaudah Equiano, a former slave

The Abolition Bill brought before parliament by William Wilberforce

French Revolution

**1791**
Slave revolt in St Domingue (Haiti)

**1794**
West India Regiment formed

**1803**
Danish slave trade abolished

**1807**
Bill to abolish the British slave trade passed

**1814**
Dutch slave trade abolished

**1823**
The Anti-Slavery Society formed

**1831**
'Baptist War' in Jamaica

**c. 1831**
French slave trade ended

**1832**
Parliamentary Reform

**1834**
Emancipation Act passed, abolishing slavery in British colonies – slaves to work 6 years' apprenticeship before receiving freedom

**1838**
Slaves in British colonies gain full freedom

**1848**
Britain adopts policy of free trade

**1865**
Morant Bay Rebellion in Jamaica

Slavery abolished in USA by 13th amendment

**1876**
Portuguese slave trade ended

**1886**
Slavery abolished in Cuba

**1888**
Slavery abolished in Brazil

**1914**
World War One begins

**1915**
Recruitment begins in British colonies

**1918**
World War One ends

**1919**
Race riots in British ports

**1939**
World War Two begins

Recruitment begins in British colonies

**1945**
World War Two ends

**1948**
MV *Empire Windrush* brings first contingent of post-war Caribbean immigrants to join the British labour force

**1952**
Legislation in USA restricts immigration from the Caribbean

**1962**
First UK legislation controlling immigration from the Caribbean

**1971**
Virtual end of black immigration to the UK

**1981**
Race riots in Brixton, Toxteth and other cities

**1993**
Murder of black teenager Stephen Lawrence

**1999**
Macpherson Report on the Stephen Lawrence Inquiry

**2000**
The Race Relations (Amendment) Act 2000

1760   1780   1800   1820   1840   1860

# Appendix

## Acts of Parliament relating to citizenship and race relations

### British Nationality Act 1948
Established the right of Commonwealth citizens to enter the UK, to work, settle and bring families.

### White Paper on Immigration from the Commonwealth 1965
Introduction of employment vouchers: 8,500 to be issued each year, largely to skilled and professional workers.

### Race Relations Act 1965
Discrimination in public places outlawed; Race Relations Board and National Committee for Commonwealth Immigrants established.

### Commonwealth Immigrant Act 1968
Anti-discrimination extended to include housing, employment and service provision; NCCI replaced by Community Relations Commission; local community relations councils introduced.

### Immigration Act 1971
Work vouchers scheme wound down and 'partiality' grandfather clause established – virtually ending all primary immigration.

### Race Relations Act 1976
Protection provided from race discrimination in the fields of employment, education, training, housing, and the provision of goods, facilities and services. The Commission for Racial Equality set up to take on a strategic and investigative role.

### British Nationality Act 1981

Three categories of citizenship established: British citizenship, and British Dependent Territories citizenship; British Overseas citizenship.

### Immigration Act 1988

1981 Act amended to incorporate free movement provision of EC law.

### Asylum and Immigration Act 1993

Asylum decision-making and appeal procedures accelerated and streamlined; in-country right of appeal introduced.

### Immigration and Asylum Act 1999

Vouchers and dispersal of asylum seekers introduced; new restrictions on illegal working imposed.

### Human Rights Act 1999

European Convention on Human Rights incorporated into UK law.

### Race Relations (Amendment) Act 2000

An amendment to the 1976 Act, and resulting from recommendations of the Stephen Lawrence Inquiry report, this legislation prohibited race discrimination in all public functions, with only a few limited exceptions. Public bodies, including the police force, are also subject to a statutory general duty to promote race equality.

# Further reading and resources

*A Salute to Black Scientists and Inventors* (Documenting Our Own History, vol. 2), Empak Enterprises (1996)

Ackroyd, Peter, *London: A Biography*, Vintage (2001). Refers to the early black population in London.

Baker, Christopher P., *Lonely Planet Jamaica*, Lonely Planet Publications (2003). Jamaica in a book.

Bush, Barbara, *Slave Women in Caribbean Society 1650–1838*, Indiana University Press (1990). Evaluates the images of slave women accumulated in published sources and folklore.

Cugoano, Quobna Ottobah et al., *Thoughts and Sentiments on the Evil of Slavery*, Penguin Classics (1999). The true story of a slave and slavery and the fight for freedom in Britain with words and debate.

Dunn, Richard S., *Sugar and Slaves; The Rise of the Planter Class in the English West Indies, 1624–1713*, W. W. Norton (1973). A portrait of English life in the Caribbean tracing the development of plantation slave society.

Dyde, Brian, *The Empty Sleeve: The Story of the West India Regiments of the British Army*, Hansib Publications (1978). The history of the West India regiments with details of military encounters.

Ferguson, James, *The Story of the Caribbean People*, Ian Randle Publishers (1999). This authoritative history contains illustrations, historical maps and a useful chronology of major events.

Froude, James Anthony, *English Seamen in the Sixteenth Century: Lectures Delivered at Oxford Easter Terms 1893–4*, Books for Business (2002). Refers to Columbus, Sir John Hawkins and the slave trade, Sir Francis Drake and the Armada.

Frow, Mayerlene, *Roots of the Future: Ethnic Diversity in the Making of Britain*, Commission for Racial Equality (1996)

Fryer, Peter, *Staying Power: Black People in Britain Since 1504*, Pluto Press (1984). Tells of the black presence in Britain.

Gates, Brian, *Afro-Caribbean Religions*, Ward Lock Education (1980). History of Caribbean religion – now out of print but available in libraries.

Graham, Ian, *The Caribbean: Country File*, Franklin Watts (2002). Geography, economy, government, transportation, education and culture of the Caribbean area.

Haynes, Aaron, *The State of Black Britain* (two volumes), Hansib Publications Ltd (1997). Takes a look at the treatment of black people through the institutions in society.

Hoyles, Asher and Hoyles, Martin, *Remember Me: Achievements of Mixed Race People*, Hansib Publications (1999). The stories of mixed race achievers, including Bob Marley, Cleo Laine and Mary Seacole.

Lewis, Matthew, *Journal of a West India Proprietor*, Oxford Paperbacks (1999). Tells of life on a plantation from a proprietor's perspective.

Majors, Richard (ed), *Educating Our Black Children: New Directions and Radical Approaches*, Routledge Falmer (2001). Analysis of the education of black children in Britain and the USA.

Murray, Robert N., *Lest We Forget: Experiences of World War Two Westindian Ex-Service Personnel*, Nottinghamshire West Indian Combined Ex-Service Association (1996). Eye witness accounts of life for black service men and women during World War Two.

Ogot, B. A. et al., *General History of Africa, vol. 5 Africa from the Sixteenth to the Eighteenth Century*. UNESCO (1999). Includes the consequences of the slave trade.

Omotoso, Kole, *The Theatrical into Theatre*, New Beacon Books Ltd (1982). A study of drama in the English-speaking Caribbean.

Pope-Hennessey, James, *Sins of the Fathers: The Atlantic Slaver Traders 1441–1807*, Castle Books (2004), previously published in 1967. An overview of the slave trade, based on the journals and letters of slave traders, merchant seamen and the slaves themselves.

Salib, S. (ed), *The History of Mary Prince, a West Indian Slave, Related by Herself*, Penguin Classics (2000). Story of a slave woman and her desire for freedom and respect.

Sherlock, Philip and Bennett, Hazel, *The Story of the Jamaican People*, Markus Wiener Publishers (1997). Tells the story of the Jamaican people from an Afro-Jamaican rather than a European perspective.

Walvin, James, *Black Ivory Slavery in the British Empire*, 2nd edn, Blackwell Publishers (2001). A thorough and very accessible study of slavery.

## Books for children

Agard, John and Nichols, Grace (eds), *Under the Moon and Over the Sea*, Walker Books (2003). A collection of poetry that conjures up the sights, sounds, tastes and tales of the Caribbean. Ideal for Key Stage 2.

Black, Clinton V., *Tales of Old Jamaica*, Longman (1988). Enjoyable stories that appeal to both boys and girls.

Brown, Stewart (ed), *Caribbean New Wave Anthology*, Heinemann International Literature and Textbooks (1990). Contemporary short stories, ideal for Key Stage 3 English.

Burke, Virginia, *Caribbean Kitchen*, Simon and Schuster UK (2001). Caribbean cookbook with recipes for the home or school.

Conolly, Yvonne (ed), *Mango Spice: 44 Caribbean Songs*, A and C Black (2001). A popular collection of Caribbean songs with CD. A good cross-curricular Caribbean musical resource for Key Stage 2.

Dash, Paul, *Traditions of the Caribbean*, Hodder Wayland (1998). An introduction to the cultural traditions of the Caribbean. Suitable for Key Stage 2.

Poupeye, Veerle, *Caribbean Art*, Thames and Hudson (1998).

Rhone, Trevor, *Old Story Time and other plays*, Longman Caribbean Writers series (1981).

## Useful websites

www.nbufront.org/html/MastersMuseums
National Black United Front (NBUF) – African contributions to technology and science

http://seacoastnh.com/arts/please022700.html
Black Heroes, White Poets – good stories, rarely told, of black history on the seacoast

5x5media.com/bhp/pages/nanny.html
Black history pages compiled by writer Emru Townsend. See page on Nanny of the Maroons

www.spartacus.schoolnet.co.uk/BlackPeople.htm
Black people in Britain

www.booksofcolour.com
Books of Colour, a non-membership book club specialising in on-line and mail order retail of books by and about people of colour

www.black-history.org.uk
Brighton and Hove Black History

http://pages.britishlibrary.net/empirehist
British Empire studies

www.bl.uk/collections/oes/caribbean
British Library Caribbean Resources on the web – Caribbean studies, history, literature, maps and sound recordings

www.brycchancarey.com
Brycchan Carey's website – 18th century black British writers. Resources for studying slavery, abolition and emancipation

www.nalis.gov.tt/Education/BIBLIOGR.htm
Caribbean children's literature: a select annotated bibliography compiled by Annette Wallace 1998

www.chronicleworld.org

The Chronicle is Britain's first internet magazine monitoring Britain's black urban communities

www.jamaicaway.com/Heroes/index.html

General website on Jamaican life and culture. See information on heroes

www.jnht.com

Jamaica National Heritage Trust – history of Jamaica with interesting archive photos

www.moeyc.gov.jm/heroes/index.htm

Jamaican Ministry of Education, Youth and Culture – Jamaica's national heroes

www.ferris.edu/news/jimcrow/mulatto

Jim Crow's Museum of Racist Memorabilia – The Tragic Mulatto Myth

www.lmal.org.uk

London's Museums, Archives and Libraries website – a listing of collections and resources to support the school history curriculum

www.100greatblackbritons.com

100 Great Black Britons – historical and contemporary figures

www.progov.uk

Public Record Office Research

www.movinghere.org.uk

Resources on migration

www.rc.umd.edu/reviews/slavery.html

Slavery, abolition and emancipation writings in the British Romantic period

# Index